OFFICIAL COPY

REMOUNT REGULATIONS.

1913.

LONDON:
PRINTED BY HIS MAJESTY'S STATIONERY OFFICE.

To Be Purchased, either directly or through any Bookseller, from
WYMAN AND SONS, LTD., Fetter Lane, E.C., and 54, ST. MARY STREET, CARDIFF; or
H.M. STATIONERY OFFICE (SCOTTISH BRANCH), 23, FORTH STREET, EDINBURGH ; or
E. PONSONBY, LTD., 116 GRAFTON STREET, DUBLIN ;
or from the Agencies in the British Colonies and Dependencies,
the United States of America, the Continent of Europe and Abroad of
T. FISHER UNWIN, LONDON, W.C.

PRINTED BY
HARRISON AND SONS, 45-47, ST MARTIN'S LANE, W.C.,
PRINTERS IN ORDINARY TO HIS MAJESTY

Price Threepence.

FIRESTEP
Editions
www.firesteppublishing.com

FireStep Publishing
Gemini House
136-140 Old Shoreham Road
Brighton
BN3 7BD

www.firesteppublishing.com

First published by the General Staff, War Office 1913.
First published in this format by FireStep Editions,
an imprint of FireStep Publishing, in association with
the National Army Museum, 2013.

www.nam.ac.uk

ISBN 978-1-908487-76-6

Cover design FireStep Publishing
Typeset by FireStep Publishing
Printed and bound in Great Britain

Please note: *In producing in facsimile from original historical documents, any
imperfections may be reproduced and the quality may be lower than modern
typesetting or cartographic standards.*

REMOUNT REGULATIONS.

1913.

LONDON:
PUBLISHED BY HIS MAJESTY'S STATIONERY OFFICE.
To be purchased, either directly or through any Bookseller, from
WYMAN AND SONS, LTD., FETTER LANE, E.C., and 54, ST. MARY STREET, CARDIFF; or
H M. STATIONERY OFFICE (SCOTTISH BRANCH), 23, FORTH STREET, EDINBURGH; or
E. PONSONBY, LTD., 116, GRAFTON STREET, DUBLIN;
or from the Agencies in the British Colonies and Dependencies,
the United States of America, the Continent of Europe and Abroad of
T. FISHER UNWIN, LONDON, W.C.

PRINTED BY
HARRISON AND SONS, 45-47, ST. MARTIN'S LANE, W.C.,
PRINTERS IN ORDINARY TO HIS MAJESTY.

Price Threepence.

THIS Manual is issued by command of the Army Council for the guidance of all concerned.

E W D Ward

WAR OFFICE,
   1st April, 1913.

(B 10410)   Wt. 5808—876   11½ M   5/13   H & S   P. 12/375

TABLE OF CONTENTS.

CHAPTER I.
THE REMOUNT SERVICE.

CHAPTER II.
DUTIES OF OFFICERS.

CHAPTER III.
ISSUE, TRANSFER AND CASTING.

CHAPTER IV.
INSTRUCTIONS FOR PURCHASERS IN PEACE TIME.

CHAPTER V.
MOBILIZATION.

CHAPTER VI.
ORGANIZATION AND DUTIES OF THE DEPÔTS.

CHAPTER VII.

REMOUNT COMMISSIONS.

APPENDICES.

DEFINITIONS.

For definitions of terms, see pp. 7 and 21.

NOTE.

Sections or paragraphs marked with a black line show where the provisional issue of Chapters II, III and V has been amended.

REMOUNT REGULATIONS.

CHAPTER I.—THE REMOUNT SERVICE.

1. *Organization.*

1. The remount service of the Army is controlled by the Quartermaster-General, through the Remount Directorate, which is a branch of his department.

2. The service consists of the following in addition to the branch at the War Office :—

  (a) The purchasing service, *i.e.*, the Inspectors of Remounts.
  (b) The administrative service, *i.e.*, the Deputy Assistant Directors of Remounts, attached to the headquarters of commands.
  (c) The depôts.

2. *Duties of the Remount Service generally.*

1. The duties of the remount service generally are to maintain the Army at its peace establishment of horses, and to prepare for its mobilization to war establishment, and its maintenance in horses while in the field.

2. Such duties include—

  (a) Purchase.
  (b) Issues.
  (c) Control of casting.
  (d) Maintenance of an equal standard in units.
  (e) Questions of shoeing and numbering.
  (f) Study of horse supply of the world for peace and war requirements.
  (g) Mobilization in horses.

3. The specific responsibility of the Remount Directorate at the War Office is detailed in the War Office Directory.

CHAPTER II.—DUTIES OF OFFICERS.

3. *Inspectors of Remounts.*

1. The Inspectors of Remounts are primarily concerned with matters relating to the purchase of horses for the branch of the service for which they are appointed, but may be required to inspect or purchase any horse.

2. They are charged with the following :—

(a) The selection and purchase of all public animals except as referred to in Section 4, 2 (f).

(b) The inspection when required by the Director of Remounts of any public horse, or proposed remount, as the representative of the War Office.

(c) The supervision of the remount depôts.

(d) The control of the issue and receipt of all animals in remount depôts in accordance with orders from the War Office.

(e) Advising the casting authority (Sec. 8, 1) as to the disposal of any horses brought forward for casting as remount cases.

(f) Any duties connected with remounts and horse organization that may be deputed to them by the War Office.

3. They have the right to enter all Government stables, by arrangement with commanding officers, for the purpose of seeing the progress made by remounts.

4. *Deputy Assistant Directors of Remounts in commands.*

1. The deputy assistant directors of remounts in commands are attached to the administrative staff of commands.

2. They are charged with—

(a) Advising and assisting command headquarters on matters generally that concern horse mobilization and remount matters generally.

*(b) The organization and supervision, under the Quartermaster-General's branch of the staff, of the classification of horses and vehicles in accordance with these regulations.

*(c) Assisting the Quartermaster-General's branch of the staff of the command, in the organization of horse impressment and horse mobilization generally.

(d) Knowledge of the horse life of their areas.

(e) Informing the War Office through their General Officers Commanding-in-Chief of the operation of foreign buyers.

(f) Purchase of horses, when so instructed by the War Office.

(g) Attendance at casting when required to advise on the disposal of non-veterinary cases.

(h) Any duty connected with horse questions that may be deputed to them.

CHAPTER III.—ISSUE, TRANSFER AND CASTING.
5. *General.*

1. No horse is to be maintained in any unit, training brigade, depôt, or establishment, that is not fit for one month's service in the field under continental conditions, with its own branch of the service. Subject to the above condition, there is no age limit.

---

* These apply in the United Kingdom only.

2. All horses on the peace establishment are considered fit and available for service, except where sick or young and untrained, and orders will be issued by the War Office for the disposal of those not serving with units of the field army.

3. Horses in depôts and training brigades, while fulfilling the above condition, are best suited to the training work required of them if a large proportion are old. Horses may be transferred to these units if the War Office approves.

6. *Issues.*

1. Units are as far as possible kept up to peace establishments, but, except in cases of small units whose training capacity is affected by shortage, remounts are usually issued in batches in October, and not as casualties occur. Remounts are normally issued from depôts, or from purchase, direct to units that require them,i n accordance with instructions from the War Office. The War Office gauges requirements from the monthly horse states of units.

2. Chargers are issued similarly in accordance with the Allowance Regulations, under War Office instructions, to officers whose applications are approved. They are issued for military purposes in the first instance, and are not to be used for general purposes till fully trained as chargers.

7. *Transfers.*

1. A charger whose return by an officer has been approved by the War Office will be returned to a remount depôt immediately, unless application is made by another officer to retain it. No unallotted chargers will be retained by a unit.

2. Applications to transfer an artillery horse to a training brigade, or to rest a horse at a depôt other than the rest depôt at Aldershot, will be submitted to the War Office by the commander of the unit concerned through the usual channels (see Sec. 11, 2).

8. *Casting.*

1. Horses and other public animals are cast from the service as unfit under three main headings :—

    (*a*) As veterinary cases, *i.e.*, for chronic disability.

    (*b*) As " Remount " cases, *i.e.*, unsuitability from various causes (see para. 2).

    (*c*) As worn out (as specified in para. 3).

2. " Remount " cases, include horses unfit by reason of being prematurely worn out (viz. under 15 years of age), wind-sucking, crib-biting, speed-cutting and brushing, stumbling and vice, those that fail to develop suitably, and horses dangerous or unsafe to ride.

3. Worn out horses are those over 15 years of age that fail to come up to the standard laid down in Section 5.

4. Horses will be cast in accordance with the general instructions laid down in the King's Regulations.

(B 10410)   A 4

5. Veterinary cases will be inspected by the assistant director of veterinary services of the command, who will record his opinion before they are brought before the casting authority.

6. "Remount" cases will similarly be inspected first by a remount officer,* who, in addition to recording his opinion, will state if he recommends retention of the horses for any other arm or service.

7. Horses other than "remount" cases incapable of further work in peace should at once be brought up for casting by the unit concerned. Remount cases should normally be brought forward for casting at the conclusion of the training season.

8. Mules and camels are cast on the same principles as horses.

9. *The disposal of cast horses.*

1. Cast horses (other than "Remount" cases) will be immediately disposed of under the orders of the command headquarters, and should not be kept a day longer than avoidable (except as detailed in the next paragraph). "Remount" cases will be disposed of directly instructions are received from the War Office regarding them. In all cases Army Form B 164 will be sent to the War Office for record after casting.

2. The casting of mares, which are free from hereditary disease, and which are considered suitable in age and conformation for breeding, will be reported to the War Office, and disposal orders awaited. The character and Veterinary History sheets should accompany the reference.

CHAPTER IV.—INSTRUCTIONS FOR PURCHASERS IN PEACE TIME.

10. *Purchase.*

1. Horses are purchased normally by the Inspectors of Remounts. Payments are usually made by the War Office on receipt of A.F. B 88. The average price is fixed by the War Office from time to time.

2. Purchasers will make out this form with the full details as specified thereon for each purchase. The form should be signed by the purchaser and the veterinary officer accompanying him.

3. If no veterinary officer is available to accompany purchasers† within the command in which they are operating, civilian veterinary surgeons will be employed, and they should countersign Army Form B 88.

---

* Normally the Inspector of Remounts specially charged with the arm in question.
† Which should be ascertained from the headquarters of the command.

4. If for any special reason a purchaser requires ready money for making purchases, application for an imprest account should be made to the Director of Remounts.

5. For facility of reference, purchasers will keep up a diary giving the exact details of their work, the number of horses seen and purchased, the names of the veterinary surgeons who accompanied them, the disposal of their purchases at the end of the day's work, and any information that may form the subject of later reference to them.

6. Purchasers' accounts should in all cases show the exact sum paid for the horse ; all contingent expenses at fairs, &c., connected with the purchase of, and applicable only to, the individual animal being shown separately. In cases where the price of the horse is quoted "to include all expenses," this fact should be clearly shown.

7. The heights without shoes, and the ages of horses to be purchased for the Army, according to their class, are given in Appendix I.

11. *Delivery.*

1. Horses, when purchased, are sent direct to units or depôts, in accordance with standing instructions from the Director of Remounts, unless orders are issued to board horses with dealers temporarily till required for issue.

2. (*a*) On purchase being made from vendors, Army consignment notes for conveyance of the horses to their respective destinations will be supplied by the Remount Officer concerned, care being taken that horses shall travel together as far as possible to obtain the advantages of lower rates. Horses conveyed together although for different destinations will be entered on one consignment note, whenever possible, but should more than one voucher be necessary cross-references should be given to obviate the payment of excess charges. The horses will travel at W.D. risk.

For scale of military rates for the conveyance of horses see Allowance Regulations.

(*b*) As regards a horse sent by vendors to a depôt for inspection, the movement will be made "carriage forward," and the charge for conveyance will be paid by the War Office. Should, however, the horse be rejected, it will be returned to the vendor "carriage forward," and the return journey will be paid for by him. No consignment notes will be issued in such cases, and public rates will apply each way. Vendors should be so informed.

3. In ordering movements by rail the following rules are to be observed by all remount officers :—

> Horses travelling in the United Kingdom should have rugs and halters, hind shoes removed, tarpaulins over trucks in wet and cold weather ; horse boxes to be used in very cold weather. Trucks should be disinfected and clean.
>
> Horses should be fed and watered immediately after a sea passage.

CHAPTER V.—MOBILIZATION.

Note.—Vehicles (other than mechanical), harness and " turn outs," are classified, impressed and purchased by the same agency as detailed herein for horses.

Note.—This chapter applies to " general " mobilization. Special instructions will be issued for " partial " mobilization.

13. *General.*

1. The mobilization of the units of the Expeditionary and Territorial Forces, and of Reserve and other units in horses is carried out, in the United Kingdom, under the orders of the General Officer Commanding-in-Chief of the command in which the units are stationed or to which they are attached.

2. No horses unfit for service (except by reason of youth or temporary sickness) are maintained in the army in peace time. In cases where the effective peace establishment is less than the war establishment, units are completed :—

(*a*) By transfer from other units under War Office or command instructions ;

(*b*) By the calling in of boarders and of horses of the reserve (*i.e.*, registered or subsidized horses) ;

(*c*) By impressment under Section 115 of the Army Act ;

(*d*) By purchase in the open market. (Chiefly in the Irish Command.)

Horses surplus on mobilization are disposed of as detailed annually by the War Office. Sick horses are disposed of under arrangements made by the Army Veterinary Service in each command, and when cured are transferred to the same destination as surplus horses.

3. Casualties occurring between mobilization and embarkation will be made good from the embarkation remount depôts.

4. It is the general rule that commands, with the exception of Aldershot, supply themselves from the resources of their own areas. In the case of Aldershot, the majority of the horses required are furnished by quotas contributed from other commands, in accordance with instructions issued by the War Office. In certain cases it may be necessary to supplement one command by a contribution from another, according to the horse population of the area. Horses to be sent to Aldershot and other large stations will be sent down by classes * direct to the various temporary horse depôts arranged to receive them, from which horses will be issued to units. Horses required for temporary duties on mobilization must be included in the general mobilization horse requirements, but will be impressed for *hire* and released later.

---

* *i.e.*, as " riders," " draught," " pack," &c.

5. *Reserve horses* consist of—

   (a) *Registered horses*—viz., those that in return for a retaining fee are voluntarily registered by their owners as available for immediate purchase by Government, on such occasions as are specified in the agreement, usually when the Secretary of State calls out Army Reservists.

   (b) *Subsidized horses*—viz., those whose owners voluntarily agree to similar terms to those described above, in return for a subsidy, which is offered for a limited number as an inducement to maintain a certain type of horse.

6. Reserve horses are primarily intended for the Expeditionary Force, and will be earmarked for the Aldershot quota unless impressed horses can be as expeditiously obtained.

7. *Classified horses* are horses classified in peace time under Section 114 of the Army Act as suitable for impressment for military purposes on emergency (see Secs. 14 and 15).

8. *Boarders* are horses on the strength of units, boarded out with private persons and liable to recall. It is assumed as a working rule that 50 per cent. are fit for immediate work, 25 per cent. as first reinforcements, and the remainder temporarily unfit.

9. Impressed purchase is based on definite figures, and lists of horses to be purchased include 25 per cent. in excess of requirements to allow of failure from various causes to produce the requisite number. Only the actual number required should be purchased unless special instructions are given to the contrary. The numbers to be sent to each unit are based on 20 per cent. being temporarily unfit or untrained in the cavalry and 10 per cent. in other arms. Units will receive remounts on this scale, and will leave behind any surplus for reserve units as specified by the War Office annually. (Sec. 18, 2). Reports are not required as to the number of the peace establishment unfit, unless it exceeds the above percentages.

10. Remounts joining on mobilization will be branded with the regimental number only after joining a unit, and will not receive an Army number at time of purchase.

11. Horses purchased on mobilization may be any age over five years provided they are fit for one year's work in the field under continental conditions.

12. All horses moving by rail on mobilization, including boarders, chargers, reserve and impressed horses, etc., must be included in the command railway programme. Horses not included cannot be moved by rail.

14. *Horse impressment (classification and preparation)*.

1. With the object of giving prompt effect to the provisions of Section 115 of the Army Act, arrangements are made in peace time for the classification and selection of horses fit for impressment on an emergency, and commands will appoint sufficient

persons as purchasers in each area to ensure the horses being impressed by the time required (see Appendix II).

2. Commands are divided into areas corresponding, where possible, to one or more petty sessional police or borough police areas. In these areas, under the supervision of the deputy assistant directors of remounts allotted to the command, the private horses are visited in their stables during the year* by officers to whom certain districts are assigned, and are classified for the military purpose for which fitted. For classes see Appendix III. The results are recorded in Army Book 389.

3. In classifying horses the following points are to be observed :—

   (a) No stable is to be entered until the owner's permission has been obtained.
   (b) Should permission be refused, the deputy assistant director of remounts of the area, or an officer detailed by the General Officer Commanding-in-Chief, will call in person and explain the law and the need for classification. Should permission still be withheld, the search warrant, allowed under Section 114 of the Army Act, will not be applied for without reference to the War Office.
   (c) The classification should aim at being a complete census of horses fit for military purposes,† but not more than fifty per cent. of the horses in any stable are to be *allotted* for impressment, unless the command is unable to find other-wise the horses required, and allotment must be distributed equally so far as possible among the owners of fit horses in the area.† Grey and white horses should be classified, but *allotted* to medical units, trains and administrative services only, except remounts for the 2nd Dragoons. All grey and white horses should be marked × in the classification list.
   (d) Tact and courtesy must be displayed towards owners.

4. Under the provisions of the Army Act the police and county associations have power to call for lists of classified horses in order that the lists may be inspected by the owners. It is, therefore, essential that these classified lists should be kept up to date in commands, and be immediately available if required for this purpose.

5. The General Officer in charge of administration in a command is responsible that the classification does not overlap. From the classification returns, specially prepared lists of stables, horses and vehicles are maintained, ready to issue to the officers and others detailed to impress and purchase on mobilization. **Only the number of horses in each stable detailed in these lists are to be purchased,** unless special orders to the contrary are issued. The observance of this order will prevent overlapping. The list should contain 25 per cent. in excess of actual requirements. (See Sec. 13, 9.)

---

* In Ireland only in certain districts.
† The horses of public bodies and food distributing trades are to be spared if possible. Single horses are an exception to the 50 per cent. rule

15. *Horse impressment (purchase).*

1. Purchase by impressment follows on the issue of a " Requisition of Emergency " by any general or field officer in command of troops for horses and vehicles required for the troops for which he is responsible. Such requisition can only be issued after His Majesty, through a Secretary of State, has declared a national emergency to exist.

2. On the issue of the " Requisition of Emergency " an officer duly authorized to collect horses or vehicles may make a demand on any justice requiring him to issue a warrant ordering the constables within his jurisdiction to impress such animals and vehicles as are specified in an attached list.

3. The constables who receive the justices' order then order the owners detailed in the schedule to furnish the animals or vehicles specified, and must accompany or precede the purchaser or collecting party.

4. The forms of requisition, demand and warrant, referred to in the above paragraphs, are provided printed together (Army Form A 2029), together with forms for the constables' order to owners.

5. As the Army Act does not compel owners to deliver their horses or vehicles at any specified spot, it is incumbent on the military authorities to collect them from the owners' premises. The owners, however, may be specially requested to send them as a help in a time of emergency, and informed that a suitable gratuity up to five shillings per horse will be paid to the civilian bringing them.

6. Purchase by impressment will be arranged in two separate systems. Horses for the Expeditionary Force, Reserve Units, and other regular corps mobilizing, will be purchased by the specially appointed purchasers, and collected by soldiers, reservists pensioners, national reservists, or such agency as may best suit the conditions in each command. Horses for the Territorial Force and Irish Horse will usually be purchased* and collected by each unit or group of units as may be arranged by divisional or other commanders concerned. The " Instructions for Purchasing Officers " (Appendix II) apply in either case, and contain instructions *re* allowances, imprest account, &c.

7. Impressed horses are inspected and purchased at certain centres, known as collecting stations, or are purchased at owners' stables and sent to these stations or direct to units, as may be ordered by commands, by officers and other persons specially selected for that purpose in peace time.† Horses are sent by

---

* The Territorial Force purchaser or other unit purchaser must be approved and definitely appointed by command headquarters.

† When a veterinary surgeon is not available at place of purchase, the purchaser must use his own judgment as to the workable soundness of the horses.

owners, or fetched by collecting parties to these centres, and thence despatched to the stations at which they are required. The price paid is fixed by the purchaser who will be supplied with a list of the average prices to be paid drawn up by the War Office. Dissatisfied owners may appeal to the County or Sheriffs' Court for arbitration as to the price to be paid, but cannot hinder the impressment of the horse.

8. Officers commanding temporary remount depôts (or officers commanding units which receive their horses direct from purchasers) will report daily, during mobilization, to command headquarters the number of horses received up to midnight the previous day, and the source whence received. This report will be sent to command paymasters.

9. Heavy draught horses will be impressed with collars and traces or chains.

16. *Steps to be taken prior to mobilization by commands.*

- 1. To admit of the prompt impressment purchase, and despatch of horses on mobilization, the following steps must be taken by commands in peace :—

(a) Allot classifying officers to petty sessional, police, and borough police areas or other classification areas.

(b) Control the yearly classification of horses.

(c) Prepare lists of allotted horses and vehicles for each purchaser, and for each Territorial Force unit or group of units which purchase their own horses and vehicles.

(d) Settle on the various collecting stations in the command and the method of collection, and prepare instructions for collecting parties if employed.

(e) Settle the system of purchase for each area. The system adopted may be that of one purchaser per area, or one purchaser to a large area with sub-purchasers under his orders, according to the condition of the district. Select local gentlemen as purchasers, or make other efficient arrangements.

(f) Arrange for veterinary surgeons to assist the purchasers.

(g) Arrange for the necessary personnel to collect and handle the horses till they reach the troops or depôt for whom destined—soldiers, reservists, national reservists, pensioners or civilians may be utilized according to circumstances.

(h) Work out with the railway authorities, rolling stock requirements and time-tables for despatch of animals to destination.

(j) Furnish command paymasters with a list of purchasing officers and their signatures, and arrange for the opening advance of £100 to each on mobilization for miscellaneous expenses.

17. *Steps to be taken on mobilization by commands.*

(*Expeditionary Force, other Regular units, Irish Horse and Reserve units, and Coast Defence areas.*)

1. On receipt of the order to mobilize the following steps will be taken by commands :—

  (*a*) Order horse purchasers to commence operations in accordance with pre-arranged plans.
  (*b*) Issue requisitions of emergency to purchasers.
  (*c*) Open an imprest account in each purchaser's name, as pre-arranged, to the amount authorized by the War Office.
  (*d*) Despatch any necessary personnel to the collecting stations.
  (*e*) Direct Irish Horse to commence purchase (viz., any squadrons that purchase for themselves).

Territorial Force.

2. Direct the commanders concerned, in accordance with Section 15, 6, to issue requisitions of emergency and commence impressment.

18. *Steps to be taken on mobilization by Regular Army units.*

1. Officers commanding units are, normally, the authority as to which of their horses other than veterinary cases are fit to take the field. There is no age restriction for the horses. Fitness to serve with their own arm for one month under continental conditions is the only condition to be fulfilled (Sec. 13, 2), but normally horses under six are not suitable.

2. On mobilization, officers commanding units will take the following steps in regard to their horse establishments :—

  (*a*) If *more* than the normal percentage of horses are untrained or unfit (Sec. 13, 9) report to the General Officer i/c Administration the number of horses of various classes required—including first reinforcement.
  (*b*) Recall boarded-out horses—50 per cent. of these are assumed to be fit for service, 25 per cent. fit for first reinforcement, remainder will be considered surplus, but may be taken into the ranks if C.Os. prefer it, instead of remounts or troop horses.
  (*c*) Transfer all unfit and surplus horses to the place previously ordered by command headquarters. (Veterinary cases are disposed of under arrangements made by the Army Veterinary Service.)

3. Officers commanding units, who receive their horses direct from purchasers and not through a temporary military remount depôt, will report daily during mobilization to command headquarters the number of horses received the previous day up to midnight, and the source whence received.

4. On receipt of remounts the following steps are necessary :—

    (a) Examine new arrivals for contagious disease as soon as possible.

    (b) Brand in accordance with regulations.

    (c) Fit harness and saddlery.

    (d) Shoe up horses.

19. *Steps to be taken on mobilization by Territorial Force units.**

1. The following steps will be taken by officers commanding units :—

    (a) Prepare and dispatch purchasing and collecting parties, with head collars and head ropes, as previously organized.

    (b) Complete requisition of emergency and demand on justices of the various petty sessional or borough police areas in which horses allotted to the unit are situated to issue their warrant to the constables to provide horses and vehicles.

    (c) Take the justices' warrant to the superintendents of police or constables of areas for signature and issue.

    (d) Direct commencement of impressment and collection.

    (e) Carry out previously organized arrangements for receipt of horses.

    (f) Examine animal for contagious disease as soon as possible after arrival.

    (g) Brand horses after joining as described in Equipment Regulations, Part III.

    (h) Fit harness and saddlery.

    (i) Shoe up horses.

2. Officers commanding units which receive their horses direct from purchasers and not through a temporary military remount depôt will report daily during mobilization to command headquarters the number of horses received the previous day up to midnight, and the source whence received.

20. *Mobilization of reserve horses.*

1. Reserve horses will be called up on mobilization by command headquarters (A.F. A 2035).

2. Reserve horses will usually be taken over by selected purchasers, as commands may arrange, at the owner's stable after the expiration of the notice required by the contract. The owner is then obliged by the terms of his contract to send them to such convenient centre, within 10 miles of their stable, as may be ordered by the command.

3. Payment for reserve horses will be made direct by the War Office, on application from the owner, who will produce his receipt from the purchaser (given on A.B. 393). The price is fixed by the agreement under which the horse is registered or subsidized.

* For units who do not purchase for themselves omit sub-paragraphs (b) to (d).

21. *Embarkation remount depôts.*

1. On mobilization, embarkation remount depôts will be formed at ports of embarkation to replace any casualties occurring since mobilization.

CHAPTER VI.—ORGANIZATION AND DUTIES OF THE DEPÔT.

22. *Control.*

1. Remount depôts and farms are directly under the control of the Inspector of Remounts in whose charge they are.

2. The superintendent of the depôt is in charge of all work connected with the depôt except the veterinary arrangements.

3. The veterinary officer is in charge of the sick lines and veterinary arrangements.

4. In the absence of the Inspector of Remounts the superintendent and the veterinary officer carry on their respective duties in co-operation, in accordance with the standing orders of the depôt and the orders of the Inspector of Remounts.

23. *Organization and duties.*

1. The organization of the depôts and farm varies with the class of horse received in each.

2. The depôts receive remounts prior to issue, horses transferred from units pending re-issue and chargers returned by officers.

3. The farms receive such horses as may be ordered to run at grass.

CHAPTER VII.—REMOUNT COMMISSIONS.

24. *General instructions for officers in charge.*

1. A Remount Commission may be organized to purchase horses, &c., in peace or in war, and being outside the theatre of operations the system is the same in either case.

2. *Officer in charge.*—The officer entrusted with the charge of an independent Remount Commission will be furnished with all the information available in the War Office, will receive special instructions, together with the names of the officers (combatant and veterinary) who are to be placed under his orders, and will proceed to the country in which his services are required.

3. *Reporting to local British representatives.*—On arrival he will report himself to the military attaché, and through him to the Ambassador or Minister accredited to that country, giving an outline of his proposals and receiving such instructions as may be considered desirable on political grounds. Any such instructions which bear on his work, or are liable in any sense to restrict his action, should be forthwith reported to the War Office.

4. He will be responsible that His Britannic Majesty's Consuls, &c., are kept informed as to the names of the officers who have the power to negotiate as to the purchase or sale of animals in any particular district, in order to prevent fraud being practised by persons who may give out that they are the agents of the British Government.

5. Failing specific orders on the subject in his instructions, he will take the advice of the military attaché on the subject of his sphere of operations, his headquarters, and his port of embarkation, which are subject to local conditions, as to which conditions he should inform himself by means of inquiry and study of reports.

6. He should give information to the military attaché, in general terms, as to persons with whom he proposes to deal, and give due weight to advice which he may receive for or against his proposals.

7. He should invariably call on H.M. Consuls in foreign countries, and request such assistance and information as they may be able to offer, which will be especially useful in countries where there is no British military attaché.

In the case of British Colonies he should at once place himself in communication with the local government and report himself to the Officer Commanding the Troops, if any.

8. *Headquarters.*—Before commencing work it is essential (*a*) To organize the commission by allotting its members to various duties, principally as district remount officers to purchase in the different districts (the principles to be followed are enumerated in detail in Appendix IV and V).; (*b*) To select the headquarters, having in view—

(1) The advantages offered by the localities and conditions of different markets for the class of horse required.

(2) The probable duration of the service.
In this connection he must study chiefly (among many other considerations)—

(3) Railway facilities.

(4) Accommodation for a central depôt.

(5) Forage and water and good conditions of climate, where such admit of any choice.

(6) Supply of labour available.

NOTE.—If the territory to be worked for his purpose is small, a central depôt will be unnecessary, and one depôt at the port will be sufficient.

25. *Embarkation ports and depôts.*

1. *Port of embarkation.*—The next matter in the order of importance to be considered is the port of embarkation.

If there should be any choice, officers will be influenced by climate, depth of water, and the shortest sea passage, as well as the points noted in Section 26.

Adequate room must be obtained for suitable means of forming a depôt, to enable an officer to collect (if there be no need for a central depôt up country), rest, sort, and detain horses before they are embarked. Horses should have at least 14 days' rest after a long railway journey, before embarkation.

2. *Depôt.*—The extent of the depôt is governed by (*a*) the average size of the ships chartered, (*b*) the supply to be furnished monthly, and (*c*) the margin necessary to be kept on hand. If one ship is to sail weekly, it is clear that to rest horses for 14 days the depôt must be large enough to contain two shiploads, and, in addition, a margin for casualties.

The latter should be calculated at 20 per cent. of the shiploads awaiting embarkation, where there is only one depôt (that at the port) ; but in large operations, where there are two depôts (one up country and one at the port) and where three ships each fortnight are despatched, the margin to be allowed at the up country or central depôt should not be less than 25 per cent., and that at the port not less than 10 per cent., *additional to* the number required from each depôt for the supply of the ships to be loaded.

26. *Despatch by sea.*

1. Unless convoy by H.M. Navy is necessary to ensure the safety of transports on the high seas, the object to be attained is the despatch of each ship without demurrage, and the carrying of her full charter load of medically clean horses in good condition and well rested for their voyage.

The absence of a good margin of supply, and insufficient provision for rest, involves demurrage of ships, which soon mounts up to a formidable item of expenditure.

2. A conducting officer and a veterinary surgeon will be sent out to take charge of each shipload.

They will probably join the commission, travelling under separate arrangements, and their services will be utilized pending the ship's departure as may be required.

Both officers should be specially employed about the ship and the cargo she is to carry, so that they may become familiar with the conditions ; and they are not at liberty to delay *en route* to join the commission.

3. All arrangements as to shipment, halters for use on board,* fittings, forage, and attendants on board ship will be made by the Admiralty through the shipping companies and their agents.

It will not be the duty of the commander of the commission to provide these, but mainly *to see that the terms of the charter are rigidly adhered to.* No ship should be allowed to sail without her proper complement of attendants.

4. A certain number of days are allowed for loading and unloading a steamer. The freight agreement will show how many. When this number is exceeded, demurrage is incurred. This is usually, in the case of ships conveying remounts, at so much per running day, and the rate is specified in the agreement.

---

* At ports outside the United Kingdom halters are to be supplied by Government.

5. While it is desirable to avoid demurrage charges, circumstances may arise in which the responsible officer must decide whether such liability should be incurred or not. In order that he may be in a position to do this, he should ascertain the actual daily rate of demurrage on each vessel.

6. *If convoy should be necessary* the remount officer in charge will take the orders of the senior naval officer on the station as to the date of despatch of ships ; in the absence of a naval officer he will telegraph for instructions to the War Office.

7. As a rule, freight will be engaged by the Admiralty in London, and it will be necessary for the responsible officer to cable his requirements to the War Office in ample time to admit of the engagement of suitable steamers.

27. *Organization of depôts.*

1. *Internal arrangement of depôts.*—The internal arrangement of depôts will vary according to the capabilities of the country, the probable duration of the service, and the extent of the supply to be furnished.

The following requirements are indispensable in the depôt at the port of embarkation :—

(*a*) Easy access to the ship.

(*b*) Sufficient cover, and paddocks fenced off to convenient sizes, for handling stock.

(*c*) Separate and adequate veterinary accommodation.

(*d*) A long "chute" or "run" (30 to 50 yards) to give easy access to horses for examination and rapid haltering.

(*e*) A well-fenced "run" to the wharf, and convenient pens near the ship, where the final veterinary examination can be made immediately before embarkation ; and, leading out of these, one or two more brows, 26 inches broad, along which horses are *led*, and mules are *driven*, to the cattle doors of the ship.

2. Where there are two depôts, that up country should have somewhat similiar arrangements but with much more elbow room ; and this central depôt should be capable of receiving all animals for prolonged treatment, while that at the port is kept as clear as possible of sickness.

28. *Despatch by rail to port.*

1. The area of purchase should, if possible, command the services of two or more railways in communication with the port.

2. The best *export* terms must be got from the railroads, and provision made for detraining stock on long journeys at feeding stations approved by the remount officer.

3. As a rough rule, stock should be detrained for 5 hours after every journey of 28 hours, and at the feeding stations they should be well supplied with water and forage. The inspection of feeding stations and the supervision of railway arrangements will be found sufficient work for at least one subordinate officer.

29. *Purchase.*

1. *Prices.*—The remount officer is responsible that the prices he pays are the best obtainable in the market. To this end he should study the market and agricultural reports, obtain advice, and attend auctions. He should deal in the open market, avoid, if possible, giving contracts, and preferably deal with a large number of persons, rather than with one or two. It is in every way desirable not to pledge the Government to take any fixed number of horses from any seller, but to give applicants permission to show a limited number of animals on a given date, on the understanding that further dealings will depend on the success of each inspection.

2. Every such order should give the exact specifications of the animals he requires, saying in minute detail what he will take and what he will not, so as to avoid subsequent complaints and mis-understandings (see specifications, Appendix V, para. 4).

3. If a broker should be employed, he should be the best available, well established, and financially strong. He should be instructed from time to time what purchases to make, and what limit of price to give. While the broker is buying, the remount officers should not deal in the same market.

4. The employment of a broker, however, is much to be depre-cated, and should not be had recourse to unless absolutely necessary. The reasons inducing the employment of a broker should form the subject of a special report, which should be forwarded to the War Office directly after the appointment. The payment of brokerage should follow the custom of the country, but under no circum-stances should it be received from both sides ; and receipts from the vendors must invariably be handed over with the animals. Care will be taken that brokerage is paid on the number of animals sold and not on their value.

5. *Freight.*—If freight is engaged by the Admiralty, contracts made for delivery at the sea-board should be at a price including all risks and expenses till the animals are approved on board ship. This is the F.O.B. (free on board) system.

6. If freight is to be arranged by the officer in charge of the commission, he may consider it best to include the purchase and through conveyance of animals in one contract with a thoroughly responsible firm. Such a contract should be either on a C.I.F. (cost, insurance, and freight) or a delivered basis. In the former case the contractor engages freight, puts the animals on board, and insures the cargo. His responsibility then ceases on his handing over shipping documents and the insurance policy to the remount officer, unless the form of contract imposes some further responsibility upon him.

7. *Contracts.*—The terms of payment require special consideration. If a contract is made on a delivered basis, the contractor is entirely responsible, and is only paid the contract price per head for each animal landed in good condition at the port of disembarkation.

8. *Travelling expenses.*—The officer commanding the commission

is responsible that the lowest rates of travelling are obtained for officers and others employed with the commission, and that the public derive all the benefit to be secured from the issue of traders or free passes on railway and steamship lines.

9. *Supplies and stores.*—When supplies (*e.g.*, forage) or stores (*e.g.*, head collars) are required in quantities, the officer, before placing an order or making a contract, should—

(*a*) Ascertain the most suitable production of the locality.

(*b*) In the case of stores, prescribe the patterns to guide supply.

(*c*) Obtain by independent enquiries, or by formal tenders, a sufficient number of offers to enable him to fix the market price.

30. *Branding and descriptive rolls.*

1. Owing to the difficulty attendant on furnishing the descriptive returns (Army Form B 88) of a shipload of horses on each ship (in large operations), copies of these need not be handed over to the conducting officer unless special orders are given to the contrary. The original Army Form B 88 should be kept by the commission.

2. All animals are to be branded on the near hindquarter with a broad arrow, and the near forefoot with numerals in hundreds ; when these reach thousands, the thousands will be branded on the off and the hundreds on the near forefoot. All animals are to be carefully shod up, before embarkation, on the forefeet only. All feet should be trimmed.

3. All animals are to be branded with an initial letter to denote nationality on the off-shoulder. The necessary brands must be ordered by the commander of the commission and be kept sharp, and are applied red hot, so that a distinct and legible mark can be ensured by one quick application, while guarding against any such injury as would result in the skin sloughing away.

31. *Correspondence and accounts.*

1. *Records.*—All business should be done in writing, and no conversation, telegram, or telephone message, which is not confirmed in writing and signed by the officer or other person concerned, should be admitted in support of any transaction. Copies of every letter and transaction must be accessible to the War Office on demand.

The officer commanding is recommended to adopt a system of registration of correspondence that will ensure all documents relating to the same service being grouped under a given head.

2. *Code.*—All telegraphic communications between himself and his officers should be in a code arranged for the purpose, so as to avoid disturbing markets by information leaking out.

3. *Accounts.*—The following four accounts will be kept by each Commission, and certified copies will be forwarded to the War Office within 7 days of the close of every month :—

(1) Cash account, Army Form A 2046.

(2) Animal account, Army Form A 2004.

(3) Store account
(4) Supplies account } Army Form A 2045.

4. *Vouchers.*—Payments will be vouched by the original receipts. A statement showing in detail all animals and stores embarked should be signed by the commanding officer of the commission, or by an officer acting on his behalf. The conducting officer on the ship should also sign this statement, and will be required to account for the animals and stores put over the ship's side. The inspector general of the lines of communication, under whom the military landing officer acts, is responsible for the safe conduct of the animals to their destination, and should account for all animals and stores taken out of the ship.

N.B.—A duplicate of the receipt given by the military landing officer to the conducting officer should be put up as a voucher to the remount depôt account at the port of disembarkation.

5. *Agreements for hire of land, &c.*—All agreements for hire of buildings, land, &c., should be legally drafted according to the custom of the country, the remount officer taking care to reserve his freedom of action, so as not to pledge his Government too far in advance, while securing right of occupation.

6. *Stocktaking.*—Stocktaking should be carried out with great care at the close of each month, showing stock on hand, purchases, shipments, and casualties, and the return summarizing the stock in each depôt, &c., rendered with the accounts for the month to the War Office (see para. 31, 3).

In addition to this, a daily stock book must be kept up in each depôt, showing daily increase and decrease in stock and casualties.

In extended operations the monthly stocktaking becomes a matter of extreme difficulty, unless the daily records are kept up very carefully.

32. *Miscellaneous.*

1. *Precautions.*—As in some countries, horse stealing and the changing of animals while in transit is very prevalent, it will be the duty of the remount officers to be specially on their guard and to take proper precautions.

2. *Private business.*—Remount officers are not permitted to purchase animals for their own use, or to enter into business relations with persons in whom they are directly or indirectly interested, without sanction obtained after a full and explicit declaration of all the circumstances, in the absence of which they will be held fully accountable. They are required to give their whole attention to the work of their Government, of whose interests they are the accredited custodians.

3. All officers are to be instructed to guard carefully against conversing with, or giving any information to, strangers on the subject of their mission, except to the extent and in the manner authorized in the exercise of their responsibility.

APPENDIX I.

SPECIFICATION OF REMOUNTS.

Troop Horses.

	At 4 years old.	From 5 to 7 years.
	hands.	hands.
Cavalry	$15 \cdot 1\frac{1}{2}$—$15 \cdot 2\frac{1}{2}$	$15 \cdot 2$—$15 \cdot 3$
Royal Artillery	$15 \cdot 2$—$15 \cdot 3$	$15 \cdot 2\frac{1}{2}$—16
Royal Engineers		
Army Service Corps...	$15 \cdot 2\frac{1}{4}$—$15 \cdot 3$	$15 \cdot 2\frac{1}{2}$—$15 \cdot 3\frac{1}{2}$
		Over 5 years.
Mounted Infantry cobs	—	$14 \cdot 2$—$15 \cdot 1\frac{1}{2}$

As a general rule, in time of peace, troop horses are purchased between the ages of 4 and 6 years.

APPENDIX II.

INSTRUCTIONS FOR PURCHASING OFFICERS EMPLOYED ON MOBILIZATION.

Also published separately for use of purchaser.

Not applicable to Ireland.

Copy issued to.., who has been appointed to the..purchasing area on mobilization for..years.

These instructions, which should be studied in peace time, come into effect on receipt of orders to mobilize from the General Officer Commanding-in-Chief of the command concerned.

It may be necessary to supplement them by instructions and information peculiar to local conditions.

> *Signature of the Staff Officer of the command who issues these instructions to a purchasing officer, and whose signature hereto constitutes the gentleman in question a purchasing officer.*

DEFINITIONS.

A *purchasing officer*, or purchaser, is the officer, retired officer, or private gentleman appointed to buy horses and vehicles on mobilization, whether impressed or belonging to the reserve, in accordance with instructions from command headquarters, and despatch or issue them to stations and units.

A sub-purchaser is a similar officer or gentleman appointed in certain areas to assist purchasing officers in the above duties, either in purchasing, or in the receipt, care, and despatch to destination of horses and vehicles.

A unit purchaser.—An officer detailed by a unit to purchase horses for that unit, or specified units, or a private gentleman specially appointed to purchase for a unit or group of units.

A collecting area.—The area from which horses are brought to an appointed collecting station.

A collecting station.—A centre to which impressed or registered horses are brought before or after purchase for issue to the force on mobilization. The collecting and entraining station are often the same.

Entraining stations.—The railway station to which horses are sent for despatch after purchase.

Reserve horses.—Horses on which the State has a lien in war time, by reason of a contract entered into with the owner, and includes registered and subsidized horses.

Registered horses.—Horses whose owners in return for a retaining fee have contracted to sell their horses to Government at the price named in the contract, if required on any emergency in which Army Reservists are called out.

Subsidized horses.—Horses whose owners agree to terms similar to those for registered horses, in return for a subsidy which is offered to induce owners to maintain a certain type of horse.

Classified horses.—Horses of private persons and firms, which have been classified as suitable for impressment for military purposes on a national emergency being declared by the Secretary of State for War, under the provisions of Section 115 of the Army Act (as amended by the Army Annual Act of 1911).

A purchasing area.—An area presided over by a purchasing officer consisting of one or more collecting areas.

A conducting party.—A party detailed from a military unit to meet and take over horses from purchasing officers.

INSTRUCTIONS TO PURCHASING OFFICERS.

SECTION 1.—*Description of impressment organization.*

1. Under Section 115 of the Army Act the military authorities have power (if His Majesty through a Secretary of State has formally declared a national emergency to exist) to impress such horses and vehicles with harness (including stable gear) as required for His Majesty's Forces.

2. It is obvious that as in modern times the outbreak of war may be unexpected and resultant hostilities follow close on the outbreak, all necessary arrangements for mobilization must be prepared beforehand,

3. With this object the classification of suitable horses in peace time for war requirements, both of the Expeditionary Force and Special Reserve, Territorial Force, has been carried out in peace time under the orders of the general officers commanding-in-chief of commands, under powers conferred by the Army Annual Act of 1911.

4. Centres, termed " collecting stations," have been organized where necessary, at which registered or impressed horses will be collected before or after purchase, as may be arranged, and thence despatched or issued to units.

5. Horses and vehicles will be collected, if necessary, at the stations referred to, and despatched to units by the officers, retired officers or private gentlemen duly appointed as purchasers, in accordance with the local plan pre-arranged by commands. Local orders will also state whether horses

and vehicles are to be purchased at the owner's stable or at a collecting station.

When possible arrangements will have been made previously for owners to send their horses to collecting stations, for which service payment to grooms is authorized.

6. Purchasers may be appointed to purchase for the Expeditionary Force, Special Reserve, Irish Horse, or for the Territorial Force, or all conjointly. In most cases, however, they will be distinct, purchasers for Territorial Force units and Irish Horse being officers of the unit, or gentlemen specially attached to a unit or group of units for the purpose.

The price of each horse, which should be the fair market price at the time, is fixed by the purchasing officer in accordance with definite data furnished by the War Office to each command from time to time.

The owner may refuse to accept, or may accept pending a reference by him to the County Court* which has the power to arbitrate on the price, but the owner cannot hinder the impressment of the horse. (If the owner accepts under protest, a note to this effect should be made on the payment order.)

7. On mobilization, the law is put into motion by the issue of a "Requisition of Emergency," signed by a competent military officer, calling on the justices to issue their warrants for the provision of horses, vehicles and harness, by the constables. An officer authorized to impress then issues his demand on the justice having jurisdiction in the area within which impressment is to take place, and the justice then issues his warrant to the constables. A constable effects the actual impressment by serving an order on the owner, and must precede or accompany the purchaser if purchasing takes place at the owner's stables, or the collecting party, if it takes place at a collecting station.

Section 2.—*Duties of purchasing officers.*

1. The duties of purchasing officers are to take general charge of the collection and purchase of the horses and vehicles in the area allotted to them.

2. Their duties include:—

   (*a*) The purchase to the extent authorized in lists supplied to them by command headquarters, of such horses and vehicles as appear to them to be fit for the service, provided horses are passed by the veterinary surgeon as workably sound for the purpose required.

   The act of purchase includes fixing the price and payment by order (like a cheque) on the command paymaster, except for reserve horses, which are paid for by the War Office.

   (*b*) Payment of a suitable gratuity, as defined in Section 5 (3), when necessary as bringing money (not to exceed five shillings per horse) to the man who brings the horses to the appointed collecting station.

   (*c*) The arrangements for branding a broad arrow low down on the near forehoof of the animal and on all vehicles purchased.

   (*d*) Affixing a label to each horse's headstall, showing class for which purchased and destination, and arranging despatch thither. See Section 6. The label should show purchaser's name, and have a note on it of any information that will help in the posting of the animals on arrival, viz., "*hunt horse*," "*quiet hack*," etc.

3. Purchasing officers for the Irish Horse and the Territorial Force units carry out the duties detailed in sub-paragraphs (*a*) to (*d*) of the preceding paragraph, under the orders of the commanders of the unit for which they are appointed to purchase.

---

* In Scotland the Sheriff's Court.

SECTION 3.—*The organization of collecting stations.*

1. The arrangements for purchase and collection must vary with the conditions of each command. General officers commanding-in-chief will select that system which best suits their own conditions. Collecting stations may be at the entraining station, or it may be necessary to have several collecting stations from which horses will be sent by batches to the entraining stations.

2. The various permissible methods are as follows (in each case the constable serves the notice on the owner in advance of or with the purchaser):—

   (i) Purchaser to be accompanied by a veterinary surgeon, and to purchase and brand each horse at its owner's stables. Horses and vehicles must then be sent, with such personnel as the purchaser may arrange, to the collecting station.

   (ii) Horses and vehicles may be brought by conducting parties by arrangement with owners, or by owners, to convenient collecting stations, where the purchaser will purchase them. There may be one collecting station or several small ones visited in succession by the purchaser.

   (iii) Horses and vehicles may be purchased at owner's stable and issued or sent direct to the unit. This will usually only apply to purchase in the London District and to the Special Reserve, the Irish Horse and the Territorial Force.

SECTION 4.—*Remuneration and terms of appointment.*

1. The following allowances are payable to the personnel employed in purchase or collection :—

Civilian or retired military purchasing officers ...	Normally £3 per diem (when an officer of any embodied unit, £1 in addition to pay of rank) and actual travelling expenses.
Civilian or retired military officers as sub-purchasers* ...	£1 per diem and actual travelling expenses.
Veterinary surgeon ...	£2 per diem (when not an officer of the Special Reserve or of an embodied Territorial Force unit). Also actual travelling expenses and allowances at the rate of 15s. 0d. per night up to 14 nights, and then 10s. 0d. per night with daily allowance of 5s. 0d. if over 10 hours, and 3s. 6d. between 7 and 10 hours, when night allowance is not drawn.
Clerks (if civilians) ...	7s. 6d. per diem ⎱ and actual travelling
Grooms, horsekeepers, &c. ...	5s. 0d. per diem ⎰ expenses.

2. If a motor car is necessarily hired the cost will be refunded. If a private car is used mileage allowance will be given under the conditions of the Allowance Regulations. The claim should be preferred by letter to command headquarters.

SECTION 5.—*Payment for purchases, &c.*

1. The assessed value of a horse or vehicle will be paid the owner by the purchaser, in the form of payment order on the command paymaster, which

---

* To assist in collection and entrainment.

order may be passed to a bank like a cheque for collection. (A book of payment order forms is in each "Purchaser's Box.")

2. No receipt need be taken from owners, but the counterfoil of the payment order book must be filled in for record.

3. A gratuity suitable to the distance brought, not exceeding five shillings per horse, may be paid by the purchasing officers to persons not in receipt of pay from Army funds bringing in horses to collecting stations.

4. Money required for the payment of bringing money, and clerks, should be obtained from the headquarters of the command by the purchasing officer. who will have an advance of £100 placed to his credit.

5. A statement of the amount expended on purchase of vehicles and horses (being a copy of the counterfoils of the payment order books) should be sent to the command paymaster, on the conclusion of the purchasing operations on Army Form N 1547 (included in the stationery box).

6. Purchasing officers are authorized to pay any necessary expenditure on the following :—

   (a) Hire of grooms for conducting parties, horse holding, &c.
   (b) Purchase of forage at local market rates at collecting stations when these are not at military stations.
   (c) Hire of stabling for horses unavoidably detrained.
   (d) Purchase of rugs, headstalls, or leading ropes when absolutely necessary.
   (e) Any minor expenditure necessarily incurred incidental to collection and despatch by rail.

7. Travelling expenses and travelling allowances should be claimed at the close of purchasing operations on Army Form O 1771. All remuneration due to purchaser, veterinary surgeons, clerks, grooms, &c., and all other miscellaneous expenditure, will be detailed on Army Form N 1531, and receipts attached for sums over five shillings.

Section 6.—*Branding and despatch of animals to units.*

1. All purchased animals and vehicles are to be branded with a broad arrow (branding irons will be issued with the stationery box), animals *low down* on the near forehoof.

2. Horses for the Expeditionary Force are usually purchased for a certain class (*i.e.* Riding, Artillery, &c.), and despatched to some appointed station or depôt by rail. Horses for Special Reserve and Territorial Force units are usually purchased for a particular unit.

3. Purchased horses and turn-outs are either issued to conducting parties sent from the unit to the collecting stations for them, or are despatched by train direct to appointed stations, as may be ordered by the command.

4. Officers commanding stations, receiving depôts, or units, to which horses are sent by rail, must be informed (by telegram) of the hour of despatch by purchasing officers.

5. At the close of each day's operations the purchaser will telegraph to the headquarters of the command the number of horses purchased that day, and destination.

Section 7.—*General.*

1. No horses should be purchased from a stable where an infectious disease has been discovered, and any such discovery should be reported at once (by telegram) to command headquarters.

2. Purchasing officers who may have to purchase reserve horses should study the terms of agreement between the Government and the owners of

" registered " and " subsidized " horses, copies of which will be found in the stationery box.

3. Failure of the owner to produce the horses contracted for should be reported at once to the Director of Remounts at the War Office.

TABLE 1.

Forms and stationery for a collecting or purchasing officer's box.

1. Army Book 390, cheque book of payment orders on the command cashier.

2. Army Book 391, consignment note (railway transport of purchases).
3. Instruction for purchasers (pamphlet).
4. Army Form N 1547, purchaser's statement of account.
5.   ,,   ,,   O 1771, form of claim for travelling expenses and travelling allowances.
6.   ,.   ,,   N 1531, statement of miscellaneous expenditure.
7. Copy of agreement with owners of reserve horses.
8. A supply of tie-on labels and stationery.

APPENDIX III.

CLASSES OF HORSES FOR THE MILITARY CENSUS.

Horses are classified for military purposes under :—

Riders.

R.1.—Horses fit for Cavalry, $15 \cdot 1\frac{1}{2}$ hands and over.
R.2.—Horses fit for Yeomanry, Mounted Infantry and pack $14 \cdot 2$—$15 \cdot 1\frac{1}{2}$ hands.

Light Draught.

L.D.1.—Horses fit for Field Artillery, 15 hands and over.
L.D.2.—Horses heavier than L.D.1, fit for transport wagons, other than dray horses, 15 hands and over.

Heavy Draught.

Shires. Clydesdales and similar heavy draught horses, 15 hands and over, that work at a walk.

Pack.

Horses and ponies that work in pack in civil life.

APPENDIX IV.

APPOINTMENT AND DUTIES OF THE COMMANDER OF A REMOUNT COMMISSION.

1. *Abstract of duties.*

(*i*) Responsibility for administration in purchase, expenditure, finance. embarkation, and discipline.

(*ii*) Allotment of the duties to officers under his command.

2. *Form of instructions.*

WAR OFFICE,
Date.....................

To..

....

1. You have been selected to proceed to..............................in command
of a commission for the purchase of

2. You will be informed later as to the names of the officers and
veterinary surgeons who will be placed under your orders.

3. The instructions of the Remount Regulations, Chapter VII and
Appendix IV, are intended for your guidance, and all documents handed to
you which bear on the work of the particular country or district to which you
are sent must be studied with attention.

4. In the administration of your commission you will follow the above
regulations and the custom of the service.

You should consult the War Office freely by telegram in case of difficulty
arising, but you must be prepared to act immediately on your own responsibility, furnishing special reports as to any deviation from order or usage.

5. On arrival at .... you should report to His
Britannic Majesty's Minister and Military Attaché, and also call on His
Majesty's Consuls or Vice-Consuls, wherever you may be.

6. You should leave England not later than..
Your departure and arrival should be reported to this office.

7. The sum of **£**........................ will be placed to your credit
with..

You will cause all officers to be paid their allowances at the rate of
£...............per diem, and their travelling claims; and your accountant will
render your accounts, after verification by you, including claims for travelling,
&c., direct to the Secretary of the War Office, enclosing all vouchers, within
the first week of each month.

8. The following are the orders for supply until further orders (see
Specification in the Remount Manual):—

Required (horses, mules, and cobs).

—	Number.	Height.	Ages.	Colours excluded.
Artillery				
Cavalry				
Mounted Infantry ...				
Transport...				
Pack				
Total ...				

Supply is to be provided at the rate of........................ ...per month
for....................months.

9. Your port of embarkation will be....................................

....

Director of Remounts.

3. *Special instructions for the commander of a Remount Commission.*

1. The commander of a Remount Commission will make the following special reports to the War Office :—

(*a*) Report as soon as possible after arrival at destination the dates by which the first and succeeding ships will be full. (It should be remembered that it is as a rule impossible to provide a ship to sail *for the port of the* Remount Commission within less than 3 weeks' notice.)

(*b*) Telegraph the departure of each ship, the total number on board, stating the numbers of each class of animal on board (whether horses or mounted infantry cobs, &c.), and the name of the officer in charge.

2. Every precaution as to the safety of all Government stock and ships must be taken ; attempts to destroy animals or hamper work by poison or violence may be expected. A careful watch should at all times be kept over stock in corrals and ships while in port. Although no actual expense may accrue to the State by damage to a ship *before* loading, the inconvenience delay, and danger which may result to work from any such attempt must be considered. The commander of the commission has discretion as to employment of detectives. Frequently this may best be done through His Majesty's Consul on the spot, but circumstances may necessitate acting independently.

8. The following reports are required from you with great regularity :—

(*a*) Monthly (by letter), general brief notes—on health, climate, operations, changes, supply, and prospects of supply, and any special information of present interest relating to staff, stock, or shipping.

(*b*) Weekly (by cable, despatched on Sunday), numbers in hand and on order ; special difficulties ; prospects of supply.

(*c*) Weekly, by letter, a brief summary of the week's doings.

4. (*a*) The commander is personally responsible for all disbursements made by himself or by his accountant (the latter, on the commander's written authority on each bill, without which no payment can be made).

(*b*) Receipts must be obtained for all moneys expended on any account whatsoever, and the receipt of the conducting officer should be given for all animals, supplies, or stores embarked at the port of departure.

(*c*) In case of "contracts" being given copies should be at once transmitted to the War Office for information, enclosing copies, with the necessary explanations.

5. The commander is authorized to employ such clerks and other labour as may be necessary for the efficiency of the commission, and also to maintain its office establishment.

4. *The final report.*

1. On the conclusion of a full and detailed report must be submitted, for which object a diary should be kept, together with copies of all reports, &c., in connection with the work of the commission.

2. The following are subjects on which a final report is required from each purchasing officer in relation to his own district or area. A *précis* is to be made by you as officer commanding the commission of all the districts supervised, with your remarks in each case.

This *précis* is to be rendered as soon as possible after the completion of the operations, each subject in the order shown.

(The report should be on foolscap paper, written on one side only, the pages and paragraphs numbered, and preferably to be typewritten.)

Every report should be carefully condensed and to the point.

For the sake of easy reference, the report on each subject should be confined strictly to the heading under which the information is being recorded.

3. (*a*) *Subjects for report.*—The place where the commission carried on its operations and the centres from which the work was carried on. If a particular officer has been to more than one country he should make his report separately on each.

(*b*) Date on which the purchasing officer left England, when he arrived, and remarks on length of passage, accommodation of ships, &c.

(*c*) Information as to the place he was ordered to, means of getting about. accommodation, railway facilities, &c.

(*d*) Persons who proved useful, how they were enabled to help.

(*e*) Persons, localities, &c., to be avoided.

(*f*) Horses: their class, advantages, disadvantages, numbers available, to what degree trained, and for what; their characteristics, staple food, style of shoeing, and at what age they are locally put into work, what sort of work that is; suitability for light or heavy draught, riding, light or heavy cavalry, &c.

(*g*) Ordinary local market prices at different ages; prevailing market conditions.

(*h*) Facilities for moving horses by rail, &c., for caring for them when bought, for embarking them.

(*i*) The class of men to be dealt with as helpers for all the operations of purchase, travelling, entraining, embarkation, &c., and the wages paid to each class.

(*j*) The best means of getting the best men.

(*k*) The best way of getting horses together.

(*l*) Finance—banks used; facilities—how payments were made; how accounts were kept; were they audited locally?

4. *General remarks.*—Under this heading the purchasing officer will note any useful information, not contained in the foregoing, for future guidance.

APPENDIX V.

APPOINTMENT AND DUTIES OF OFFICERS OF A REMOUNT COMMISSION.

FORM OF ORDER OF APPOINTMENT OF AN OFFICER ATTACHED TO A REMOUNT COMMISSION.

WAR OFFICE,

Date............................

To..

1. You are directed to proceed to..
to join the Remount Commission, under...,
for general duty, as the officer commanding may direct.

2. You should report details as to your departure from England by letter to the War Office, and you are required to start as soon as possible after receiving an imprest for £............ , and you will make your own arrangements as to passage.

3. You will produce this letter as authority for joining the commission, when the officer commanding will give you further instructions as to the nature of your employment, and you must distinctly understand that you will be under his orders, and that you are to report yourself without delay, after disembarkation.

4. You will not wear uniform, *or in any way indicate the nature of your duty*, or the object of your journey, from the time you leave England until you have reported yourself at...........................

5. All your accounts, claims, reports, and correspondence will be submitted to the officer commanding the commission to which you are attached.

6. Your duties are described in Chapter VII and Appendix V of the Remount Regulations.

....

Director of Remounts.

INSTRUCTIONS FOR WORKING A REMOUNT DISTRICT.

1. *General instructions.*

1. The territory to be worked should be divided into districts, and these should be so accurately defined as to prevent one remount officer trespassing on another purchaser's ground, an error which would tend to raise the market price by competition.

A district remount officer will, within certain well-defined lines, be given a free hand in his district, but will not be permitted to make any arrangements likely to affect the remaining districts without the sanction of the officer commanding the commission.

For purposes of finance it should be borne in mind that the same maximum price will not necessarily be paid in all purchasing districts of a large country. The actual market value of the animal will, in some remote districts, be lower than in others which are more accessible ; and when the cost of freight, &c., has been taken into account, the purchase price of the animal, plus all charges up to the time of delivery at the central depôt, should not exceed the maximum price fixed at headquarters by the officer commanding the commission.

2. The settlement of a standard maximum price at the headquarters of the commission does not absolve the district remount officer from making fresh suggestions and using efforts to raise the quality of the stock purchased and to reduce the prices paid—it is in this that he must be allowed a free hand ; but no action should be definitely taken without consultation with headquarters, inasmuch as the full knowledge of all the circumstances of all the districts is there.

3. It is the business of the district remount officer to be constantly moving about and making enquiries on such days as are not devoted to purchasing duties.

4. The district remount officer must keep duplicate copies of all reports, transactions, and notes of interviews.

5. To curtail expenses, no travelling or change of station outside his own district is admissible without sanction from the officer commanding, which, with other details, should be conveyed by means of periodical headquarter orders signed by the officer commanding and kept for reference.

2. *Purchase from dealers.*

1. In order to avoid any possibility of misunderstanding between the purchaser and the dealer, a specification (based on somewhat the following terms) should be given to every dealer having permission to collect animals, alterations being made to meet special requirements or local circumstances.

Place...

Date...................................

SPECIFICATIONS FOR HORSES OR COBS.

Example: for active service.—Height (without shoes) :—

Class A.—15·$\frac{1}{2}$ hands to 15·3 hands.
,,   B.—14·2$\frac{1}{2}$,,   15   ,,
,,   C.—14·1   ,,   14·2$\frac{3}{8}$,,

Age.—5 years to 9 years.

Riding cobs (not ponies), geldings and mares (not in foal), in fair flesh and condition, able to carry 15 stone under active service conditions.

Sound in action, wind, eyes ; practically sound otherwise.

Strong, active, and sufficiently fast.

Fair riding shoulders, strong quarters and loins.

Good constitution.

Short, well-shaped backs and legs.

Roomy, well ribbed.

Good, clear, straight action.

Strong, clean legs and feet, properly shaped and placed.

Quiet, without vice, well broken, and mouthed.

Teeth complete, well shaped, not tampered with.

Colour, not very light grey or white.

The remount officer is the sole judge as to suitability.

(Signed)................................

Remount Officer.

2. The dealer should be told that the following, among others (which are obvious), are grounds for rejecting any horse, no matter what his other conformation may be :—

   (*a*) Small, weak quarters.

   (*b*) Flat sides (having due regard, however, to the country in which they are bought).

   (*c*) Long, weak, bending pasterns.

   (*d*) Split up and leggy, or both.

   (*e*) Small joints.

   (*f*) Close hocks or action.

   (*g*) Legs not being well placed.

   (*h*) Any mark of brushing which is *not* clearly due to bad shoeing.

   (*i*) Any indication of weak constitution.

   (*j*) Very straight pasterns.

   (*k*) Small or uneven feet.

   (*l*) Vice of any kind.

   (*m*) Evidence of fistulous withers.

   (*n*) Evidence of any operation in the teeth.

   (*o*) Bad condition.

   (*p*) Parrot mouth or undershot.

   (*q*) Capped elbows.

   (*r*) Marks of whip or spur, not done under the eye of the inspector, or undue sweating, being probably indicative of vice or bad manners.

   (*s*) Very short docks.

3. *Example.*—In arranging *prices*, the dealer must be shown exactly what he is expected to pay for, somewhat under the following terms :—

Place.....................................

Date...........................

The dealer's tender price per animal includes :—

   (*a*) Every expense of every kind connected with inspection, and up to and including safe delivery (alive and without injury which would render an animal permanently unserviceable), at..........................., to an agent of the British Government.

Exceptions :—

Provision of branding irons.

Rail and personal expenses of remount officers.

Feeding. See sub-para. (*c*).

(b) Animals must be accompanied on a railway by a competent man, and must be detrained, fed, and well watered at least every 28 hours; when entraining or re-entraining animals, each car to be provided with......bales of hay. Not more than......animals to each car.

(c) Dealer takes charge of, and responsibility for, Government animals, and feeds them at a rate of......per diem until entrained on any date specified by a duly authorized officer. This price to cover only hay and water feeding. No payment is made for day on which animals are entrained, as the dealer is paid for feed on the first day of purchase.

(d) Dealer provides inspection ground, labour and everything necessary to enable the remount officer to purchase about 100 animals per diem, *i.e.*, a minimum of..... riders, ... leaders, ... branders, ... blacksmiths, ... clippers, ... ropers or assistants, &c., one clerk, a forge, branding chute, covered veterinary shed (unless forge be suitable),5 pens for stock,300 yards gallop,clipping machine,tail shears, scissors, saddlery, ropes, slips ; *conveyance for inspecting officers from and to rail station or hotel, on payment ;* calkins and shoes removed, feet trimmed, and, if necessary, re-shod in front with flat shoes ; long hair removed from jaws, heels, legs, withers. A veterinary surgeon (with brands) accompanies the remount officer. The remount officer is the sole judge of any matter connected with inspection of animals. Payment is made by cheque from .... when animals are safely delivered at ....

(Signed)...........................
Remount Officer.

3. *Corrals and inspection grounds.*

1. Where the demand is large, and the inspections are to take place in open country, the following specifications are suggested for corrals and for the appliances which are necessary for convenient and rapid work ; and the dealer will require to know this in advance, otherwise much time will be lost for the remount staff :—

Specification for corrals or inspection grounds for handling horses and mules.

2. All to be of the strongest material and to be constantly disinfected.

Strong, well-built corrals.
Paddocks for inspection, with good water and feed.
Collecting pens.
Two chutes for bridling.
" Temporary reject " pen.
Pen for " Rejected " horses.
Pen for " Accepted " horses.
Gallop—300 yards long.
Forge and appliances.
Branding chute, strongly constructed.
Veterinary inspection pen.
Entraining pens.

The inspection ground to be close to railroad, and not nearer than ...... miles to the city limits of .... (as a precaution against infection).

Minimum labour required at each inspection :—

1 foreman.
3 riders for 100 horses, and not less than 5 if 100 is exceeded.
1 leader for every rider.
1 blacksmith.
3 branders and clippers.
6 helpers.
1 clerk.

(*a*) Horses are to be caught up and haltered at least one hour before the inspection commences, and kept perfectly quiet.

(*b*) The remount officer will decide whether horses are to be ridden barebacked or in saddles.

(*c*) Only snaffle bridles will be allowed.

(*d*) Riders will be required to saddle, mount, and dismount unaided in the presence of the inspector.

(Signed) ....

Remount Officer.

4. *Form of order to dealer for collection of horses or mules.*

Order No. ....

Date ....

Under specifications dated ....

Messrs. ....

A remount officer will be at .... on ...., and, pursuant to your request, you are granted permission to collect and submit for his inspection .... for sale to the British Government.

You must distinctly understand that, should circumstances over which I have no control prevent inspection, the British Government will not hold itself responsible for delays, and any collection of animals will be entirely at your own risk.

The remount officer will only select such animals as come exactly within the specifications quoted, and *will not inspect more animals than the total number which you have been permitted to collect*, which is given above.

This order to be shown to the remount officer.

Signature of Officer
Commanding the Commission ....

5. *Form of orders for remount officer deputed to inspect dealers' stock.*

1. *Printed on the back of above order.*—You will not commence inspection before this order has been placed in your hands.

2. Directly the inspection is finished you will return this order to headquarters, with the following entries completed, which must tally with those in the Inspection Book (see Sec. 6).

Report of inspection.

(A) Began inspection ....

(B) Purchased, Class A (price ....).

        ,,   B (,, ...).

        ,,   C (,, ...).

        Total (,, ...).

(C) General quality shown ....

(D) Any undue number of rejections ....

(E) General remarks ....

....

(F) Date of returning this paper
        to headquarters ....

Signature of officer
carrying out the
inspection. ....

33

6. *Inspection Books.*

1. *With every dealer* there should be left a book containing all information as to work actually done at an inspection, signed by both remount officer and veterinary surgeon, and showing (*a*) the date, (*b*) the number of the animals taken in each class, and (*c*) the foot-numbers used, (*d*) the details of consignments, (*e*) and stock purchased but temporarily left on hand, sick, &c., so that, if owing to illness or other cause, a different officer should continue to inspect at that place he may know exactly what has occurred on the occasion of the last visit and what special orders (if any) were given at the time.

The dealer's accounts should be verified from this book, and countersigned by the inspecting officer before being sent to headquarters for payment, and where the bills will be again checked by the document described in Section 5.

These books should be collected and returned with all papers at the close of the commission.

2. Where there is more than one purchasing station, the *foot-numbers* to be used at that particular station must be given in advance to each separate officer, so that by reference to these numbers the exact locality of purchase, the date, and the officer concerned may be identified at any time.

7. *Duties of officers concerned in purchase operations.*

1. To prevent misunderstanding, the various responsibilities of remount officers and veterinary surgeons are thus defined :—

The duties of the remount officer :—

(1) Discipline and general management of an inspection, on the lines laid down by the head of the commission.
(2) Decision as to conformation, size, quality, and action of any animal.
(3) The suitability of the animal to the needs of military service.
(4) A general supervision of the limits of age, wind, &c.
(5) When there are different classes of animals, classification as to service and price.

Note that it is necessary that (4) should be taken concurrently with (2) in order to arrive at a just estimate of (5).

(6) The careful supervision and management of rail and other expenses and arrangements inside his district.

2. The duties of the veterinary officer or surgeon are :—

(1) Health, sanitation and soundness in every particular, and the recording of correct ages.
The veterinary officer should be so placed while the work progresses, that he may have an opportunity of conferring with the inspecting officer.
(2) While active consultation is much to be desired on all subjects, it must be remembered that the responsibility for soundness is the only responsibility incurred by the veterinary surgeon, and his decision is final, and is attested by his signature on the Army Form B 88, and in the Inspection Book.

3. The duties of the superintending officer of a depôt or corrals are :—

(*a*) Entraining and detraining stock, making all needful railway arrangements, and the conveying of animals on arrival to their pastures, and to the railway for entraining.
(*b*) To follow up by telegraph and letter all losses or damage by rail, until the matter be settled, keeping all correspondence.
(*c*) To control the sufficiency and quality of forage, the sufficiency of the reserve of the same in the event of bad weather ; and to see to the state of the water supply and efficient working of windmills, engines, &c., in use for this purpose ; the state of the fences, hay racks and feed troughs, and to ensure that there should be no nails, barbed wire, loose woodwork, or anything tending to damage of stock in any part of the ground, &c., occupied by the depôt.

APPENDIX VI.

APPOINTMENT AND DUTIES OF THE EMBARKATION OFFICERS OF REMOUNT COMMISSIONS.

1. *Abstract of duties.*

I. To check measurement of fitted ships.
II. To fit those which require fitting.
III. To supervise replacement of fittings which have been removed or damaged on a previous voyage.
IV. To superintend loading.
V. To supervise generally and, in conference with agents, deal with shipping arrangement.

2. *Form of instructions.*

WAR OFFICE,

Date.......................... ....

To..

....

1. You have been selected to proceed to..
for duty as embarkation remount officer.

You will leave for that port by the most expeditious route not later than..., making your own arrangements as to passage on receipt of an imprest for £.......................

2. You will report to this office by letter your departure from England.

3. You will produce these instructions to...
...., commanding the Remount Commission in.., in proof of your identity.

His official address is ....

4. Uniform will not be worn in any foreign country, and you are to regard your mission as being of a strictly confidential nature.

5. While at.. your services are at the disposal of the officer in command of the Remount Commission, for any duty for which you may be detailed.

6. Your duties are outlined in Appendix VI of the Remount Regulations.

....

Director of Remounts.

3. *Duties.*

1. The duties of the embarkation remount officer are as follows :—

(*a*) To ensure that all ships are fitted strictly in accordance with the latest regulations on the subject, of which you are given a copy, and the measurements must be tested by yourself.

(*b*) To see that all fittings are sound and serviceable, and present no dangerous surface.

(*c*) To see that the ship is perfectly clean, the alleyways clear, and ready to be loaded, before you pass her for this service.

(*d*) To see that animals are properly sheltered from wind and weather and escapes of steam.

(*e*) To carry on all correspondence with the ship's agents, in reference to all matters which may arise, as the representative of the officer commanding the commission.

(*f*) To make sure that the water supply is accurate, and that the supply of forage when passed for the ship by the inspecting veterinary officer is properly embarked.

(g) To see that the stores and appliances required to be carried by the ship for the remount service are in good order, and on board.

(h) To report the ship ready for loading; to superintend the actual work of loading as the animals pass from the brows to the ship, and their convenient stowage on board; and to sanction the allocation of the stalls, &c., for animals, fowls, &c., intended for food.

(i) To inquire as to the presence of the ship's crew, and not to permit loading until satisfied on this point.

(j) To ensure that arrangements have been made as to the correct number of muleteers and foremen being embarked.

(k) To select the foremen, in consultation with the ship's agents.

(l) To see that officers' accommodation, lavatories, &c., are in proper condition for occupation before final inspection of the ship.

(m) To inspect the accommodation, and direct the quartering of the muleteers.

(n) To convey to the ship's captain any special written directions which may be necessary.

(o) To give the order for the ship to leave the wharf as soon as possible after the last animal is embarked.

(p) To control the admission of strangers to the wharf and to the ship.

2. The embarkation officer will report direct to the commander of the commission, and take his views on all matters connected with the duties to be carried out.

Any suggestions, &c., should be made to him and not to the War Office.

3. The embarkation officer will keep a list of the ships notified to arrive for transport service, and keep in an " embarkation book " all notes connected with each ship, her cargo, attendants, and crew, as she sails, with a view to furnishing information when required as to the various points under his control; the class and efficiency of the muleteers; questions specially raised by the agents, &c.; and will bring to light any violation of stipulations (such as the ship not carrying a doctor, should the number of the crew require it), &c.

4. The following points should receive particular attention when inspecting or loading a horse transport :—

(a) The shipping agent should be present in person to attend the commanding officer. It is not sufficient that his stevedore who has charge of the loading should be the only person to represent the firm.

(b) The width of the brows and "runs" leading over the wharf should be carefully inspected; 26 to 28 inches is sufficient, and should not be exceeded in any part of the brow or "run," so that animals may have no room to turn round.

(c) The windsails should be rigged and trimmed, and properly made fast below, at the final inspection of the embarkation officer *before loading*. He will then have an opportunity of judging of their condition. The ship will be the better for the ventilation, and then there will be no danger to be apprehended from the sudden arrival of a squall during or after loading.

(d) Attention to be paid to the length of the windsails and to the casing of the electric fans. No electrical appliance should be considered satisfactory which does not fulfil all the duties required of it, in ventilation and lighting *simultaneously*. The embarkation officer can best judge of this by seeing the fans, &c., at work, shortly after the ship's arrival at the port, so as to give time for alterations being made if required.

(e) Water barrels should be full when the final inspection is made, and all spare timber properly stowed, and tarpaulins on the upper deck made fast, ready for sea.

(*f*) Officers should be posted in the most necessary parts of the ship to supervise loading, and to stop smoking, except on the upper deck.

(*g*) The conducting officer and the veterinary surgeon detailed to sail in the ship should be present throughout the whole of the loading.

(*h*) The shipping agent should provide that no strangers are admitted to the ship during loading. It is also desirable that the captain should be on board the night before sailing.

(*i*) The embarkation officer should insist that the ship shall leave the wharf the moment the last animal is on board. The muleteers should be taken on when the ship has swung clear of the wharf.

5. The following information must be carefully recorded by the embarkation officer in his notes, and the necessary entries made on the Admiralty Maintenance Form by him (see " C " of Appendix X):—

(*a*) He will note that in making the entry for " Maintenance " on the Admiralty return of embarkation, if a ship is late and not able to keep her date as notified to him from the War Office, the date on which the freight could *have been ready, had the ship kept her time*, is to be invariably entered.

It is to be observed that the arrangements are to be so made in advance, that the cargo of every ship should be ready for her specified date, and it is to be assumed that it *will be so ready* unless the embarkation officer is informed to the contrary, by the officer commanding the commission.

(*b*) The embarkation officer will further note, that as long as discretion is allowed, by charter, to the "remount officer at the port of embarkation," the *load of a ship is to be limited to what she can carry with safety* in the opinion of the officer commanding, or his representative. The fittings of the ship for ventilation will have an important bearing on this ; and it is for this reason that these are to be ordered to be in full working order at the time of the final inspection.

The remonstrances which may arise on this subject, on the part of the shipping agents, are not to influence any officer in acting *on his responsibility*, to the best of his judgment, and in consultation with the staff.

But in any case where a ship is sent to sea with *less than her load as indicated in the charter*, very full explanations must be given as to the reasons which prevented her carrying full number, giving measurements and the numbers carried on *each deck*. In all cases the measurements are to be made most strictly and exactly, according to regulation.

6. Unless there is any exception made in the charter, a ship carrying 100 passengers should have a doctor on board.

7. Unless there are orders to the contrary, a clause should be inserted in the ship's articles that muleteers, &c., will not be allowed to land at the port of destination, and this should be explained to all hands before they sign on.

8. A certificate will be obtained by the embarkation officer before each ship sails (and forwarded to the officer commanding the commission) from the veterinary officers concerned in the embarkation, that *every horse has been examined immediately prior to shipment*, and that the animals are, in their opinion, free from infectious or contagious diseases.

9. The foremen and muleteers are entitled to reasonably good accommodation, to which shipping agents are not always disposed to give proper attention.

They should be searched for arms, if embarked in a foreign country : arms, if found, can be handed over to the ship's captain, a receipt being given.

If coloured men, as well as whites, are taken on, the races should be quartered separately, in the interests of discipline.

10. All stores (including horse clippers) are to be provided and placed on board under the recommendation of the senior veterinary officer and under the sanction of the officer commanding the commission.

....

Director of Remounts.

APPENDIX VII.

APPOINTMENT AND DUTIES OF CONDUCTING OFFICERS.

1. *Abstract of duties.*

A. To take charge of the animals handed over at the port of embarkation.
B. To account for them at the port of disembarkation.
C. To be responsible for the discipline of the muleteers and the allotment of their work.
D. To arrange, in conference with the veterinary surgeon, for the feeding and watering and care of the animals.
E. To settle the hours of work.
F. To take the necessary precautions against fire.
G. To furnish the voyage reports.
H. To submit reports on the efficiency of the veterinary surgeon and men under his orders.

2. *Form of instructions.*

WAR OFFICE,

Date.......................

To..

....

1. You are detailed to take charge of a remount transport proceeding to... from......................................., and you will leave for the latter port by the most expeditious route not later than..., making your own arrangements as to passage on receipt of an imprest for £...........................

2. You will report to the War Office, by letter, your departure from England.

3. You will produce these instructions to..., commanding the Remount Commission at..., in proof of your identity.

4. Uniform will not be worn in any foreign countries, and you are to regard your mission as being of a strictly confidential nature.

5. While at...................................... your services are at the disposal of the officer in command of the Remount Commission for any duty for which you may be detailed.

6. Your duties are outlined in Appendix VII of the Remount Regulations.

....

Director of Remounts.

3. *Duties of a conducting officer.*

1. The conducting officer will check the number of animals embarked and *make sure that he has ascertained the correct number on board* before signing any receipt for same. A detail of the numbers of animals on board will be

prepared in triplicate on Army Form G 1033. One copy of this form will be
signed by the conducting officer and handed over to the commander of the
commission, to whose account it will form a voucher for striking the animals
off charge. The remaining two copies will be signed by the officer
commanding the commission, and will be retained by the conducting officer
for disposal in accordance with para. 3.

2. Supplies and stores embarked will be checked by him, and the receipt
handed over to the officer commanding the commission to be used as a
supporting voucher to his accounts.

3. *Voyage report.*—On arrival at the port of disembarkation he will hand
over his animals, taking a receipt for them from the military landing officer
or the officer to whom he finally handed over his charge. This receipt will
be taken on the copies of the voucher in his possession, under para. 1,
any necessary explanation of the difference between numbers embarked and
landed being inserted on the voucher, casualties being supported when
possible by the certificate of a veterinary officer. One copy will be retained
by the officer receiving the animals, and will be the voucher for bringing the
animals on charge in a land account.

4. He will render to the military landing officer a report of his voyage
(see attached form), taking his receipt for the same.

5. Under the head " Casualties " he will account for the exact difference
between the number of animals he embarked and the number for which
he obtained a receipt on disembarkation.

6. It does not come within his province to comment on the "class" or
"quality" of his charge, but he will limit himself to the " condition " in which
they are embarked or disembarked, having in view all the circumstances
which may affect, or appear to affect, conditions adversely.

Every case of objection as to condition should be brought to the notice of
the remount officer at the port of embarkation during the shipment of the
animals, in order that the conducting officer's adverse criticism may be made
the subject of enquiry.

In reporting adversely, remarks must be specific, and not of a general
nature.

7. He will make a separate and special report on the foremen and
muleteers sent on board his ship, for the information of the officer commanding the commission.

8. At the port of disembarkation he will report himself in writing to the
base commandant for further orders. Any case of excessive loss or apparent
neglect will be brought to the notice of the War Office.

9. All conducting officers will provide themselves with the latest edition
of the Regulations (see Appendix VII), and special attention is called to the
paragraphs therein relating to " feeding," " watering," and " management of "
horses on board ship.

10. Horse clippers placed on board ship are to be handed over, with the
spare veterinary and other stores, to the officer detailed for the purpose at
the port of disembarkation, accompanied by a detail in duplicate of the actual
quantities. One copy of this detail, duly receipted, will be retained by the
conducting officer ; the other copy will be the voucher for bringing the stores
on charge in a land account. Spare supplies will be similarly dealt with.

11. Heavy-coated horses should be clipped during the voyage if his
instructions require it.

12. After having handed over his horses (or mules) at the last port of disembarkation, and failing other instructions from the War Office, the
conducting officer will return to England as soon as a passage can be provided
for him, and report himself to the War Office immediately on arrival,
for further instructions.

4. *Notes on routine duties on remount freight ships.*

1. Foremen, assistant foremen, two carpenters, and the muleteers are
under the orders of the conducting officer, and the feeding and the work done
by them are under his direction.

The captain of the ship is responsible in all cases for discipline relating to the safety of the ship.

No smoking to be allowed between decks.

Night watchmen to be carefully selected and made to report every hour to the ship's officer on the bridge.

2. Care to be taken that the animals have plenty of water, and in the hot weather, especially, water should be given the last thing at night.

3. All feeding troughs to be taken off at night.

4. *Ventilation.*—Wind sails and ventilators to be carefully watched and trimmed *by the ship's crew*, at the request of the conducting officer, made personally to the officer on the bridge.

Cattle doors to be closed at night when the weather is cold. Animals not to be exposed to too much draught..

5. The following daily routine is recommended, but can be altered by the conducting officer, and he must remember that *abundance of water is of the highest importance :—*

6 a.m.—Water.
6.30 a.m.—Hay and feed.
8 a.m.—Men's breakfast.
9 to 11 a.m.—Clean out and groom horses.
11.30 a.m.—Water and feed with hay.
12 noon.—Men's dinner.
1 to 3 p.m.—Get up forage for next day and groom horses.
3.30 p.m.—Water and hay up.
4 p.m.—Men's tea.
5 p.m.—Feed and hay.
8 p.m.—Water and hay.

6. *Veterinary.*—*Conducting officers* will be held responsible that all surplus drugs and veterinary stores are handed over in good condition by the veterinary surgeon of the ship to the landing authority at the port of disembarkation.

A duplicate list of the instruments and drugs put on board each ship will be given to the conducting officer by the embarkation officer.

7. *Forage.*—Forage is found under the charter by the shipping company, and an ample quantity is placed on board, consisting of the estimated ration for the voyage, plus a considerable margin to allow for delays and accidents, details of which should be received from the embarkation officer; but in view of the possibility of difference of opinion arising with the ship's officers, with the object of economising unduly the supply of forage, the conducting officer is warned confidentially that *he* is responsible for the feeding, and that if any such difference arises with the master of the ship on this point, *the conducting officer's orders are paramount.*

8. *Ties.*—Officers must be careful to keep all horses tied up short, to prevent them biting one another.

9. *Feeding.*—For the first two days the feed should consist of hay only, and for the remainder of the first week two small feeds of oats and bran can be added daily ; for the remainder of the voyage the grain is to be given in three feeds daily. A supply of hay ought to be always kept in front of the animals.

10. *Veterinary officers.*—The veterinary officer is entirely responsible for the medical and other treatment of the sick animals, and while it is his duty to advise, with the conducting officer, in regard to the feeding and hygienic care of the animals generally, any complaints that he may wish to make or alteration to suggest must be made by him to the conducting officer, and not to the ship's captain or officers.

11. *Sanitation.*—The ship ought to be thoroughly "mucked out" once weekly at least, during the voyage, while being carefully cleaned daily.

Dirt or obstruction of every kind is to be prevented from passing to the scuppers. Sufficient men are to be detailed to be constantly going round all horse decks and keeping scuppers clear, and the conducting officer will satisfy himself by frequent personal inspections that they are clear and working freely.

12. *Temperatures.*—The same animals should not be left for long in any part of the ship where the temperature ranges high and the ventilation may be less satisfactory. They should be constantly shifted and replaced by others. Such unfavourable parts of the ship should be the subject of constant investigation.

13. The conducting officer is reminded that he is personally responsible that the best possible care is taken of the animals on board. He may have a rough untrained lot of muleteers to deal with, but must remember that the engagement of these men is made with all care that can be given to it by His Majesty's Vice-Consul in communication with the remount officer at the port, and that they are the best available of their class. The foremen are specially sought after with a view to getting the best men possible.

Reports are generally favourable to a mixed crew, white and black, as, being quartered separately, it is found that the men of one colour will not join those of another if trouble should arise.

The best way to get the work done is by personal effort and example, and by being unremitting in attention to watering and feeding, and visiting both by night and day at uncertain hours.

14. All hands should be searched for arms before admission to the ship. If any are found they can be handed over to the captain, and a receipt given to the owner.

Cases of mutiny and fire have occurred on board horse transports, and therefore the conducting officer must never relax his supervision over his men, and must be prepared to act energetically if occasion should arise.

The following are the orders to be observed and the precautions to be taken against fire on transports during loading, &c. :—

(1) The conducting officer will visit and make himself familiar with his ship on a day prior to loading, and will be required to be present during the whole loading.

(2) No smoking is allowed on board the ships between decks. Any person caught smoking is to be put off the ship.

(3) Precautions against fire are taken by the captain and officers of the ship, and will be observed by the conducting officer, both at sea and in port.

(4) Strict orders are given to the watchmen who are on duty, while the ship is alongside the wharf, to allow no smoking on the wharf or near the ship. The ship's quartermaster is also on duty to stop any smoking except in places set apart on the upper deck.

(5) The remount officers (one on each deck) will have instructions to enforce the rules.

(6) It is generally advisable for the ship to anchor away from the wharf directly the last horse is embarked, and to take muleteers on board there. The muster roll of the muleteers is given to the conducting officer by the embarkation officer while the ship is thus at anchor and when the men are all on board. The muleteers are told off to watches, and foremen assigned before the ship sails, and the fire and emergency stations will be assigned and written notices distributed about the ship.

5. *Form of report to be made by the conducting officer on the disembarkation of horses (or mules).*

Voyage report.

From the hired ship.............................., on its voyage from....................
to........................

[This report is to be filled up in duplicate, accompanied by a separate report from the veterinary officer or veterinary surgeon on professional matters, and handed to the military landing officer for the information of the General Officer Commanding the District or Station, who will transmit them to the War Office without delay.]

1st

Embarkation ...	Port ... ...
	Date of embarkation... ...
	Date of sailing ... ...
	No. and kind of animals ...

Arrival at and sailing from other ports	Port ... ...
	Date of arrival ... ...
	Date of sailing ... ...

Disembarkation	Port ... ...
	Date ... ...
	No. of animals ... ...
	Condition of animals ...

Number of days on the voyage ... ...
2nd. Remount officer in charge ... ...
    ,,   ,, assisting ... ...
  Veterinary officer or veterinary surgeon ...
    Qualification ... ...
    Terms of engagement ... ...
3rd. Ship's officers and crew (assistance, if any, given by)—
4th. Fittings, type of, and report thereon—
5th. Drainage—
6th. Ventilation—
7th. Lighting—
8th. Water—
9th. Forage—
10th. Attendants—
11th. Weather—
12th. Casualties and general health—
13th. Routine of duties (day and night)—
14th. General remarks (if any)—

[Any special report necessary on points not covered by this form should be made on a separate sheet and attached to the form.]

Dated at..........................., this ....day of ....

Signed ....

APPENDIX VIII.

DESPATCH OF REMOUNTS BY SEA.

See also Appendices IX, XXI (Tender and outfit scale, horses), X, XXII (Tender and outfit scale, mules) of the Regulations for H.M. Transport Service.

NOTES ON SEA TRANSPORT.

1. *Freight ships generally.*

1. The transports and freight ships required for the service of transport from home and from the countries in which Remount Commissions are serving to the theatre of operations are chartered, and their fittings are prescribed under Admiralty regulations ; and all ships sailing from home ports would be prepared in accordance with the same.

2. During the course of a war, ships may have to be taken up for instant service while lying in other than home ports, and they would therefore have to be fitted under the supervision of the officer in charge of the Remount Commission abroad. He should be provided with Admiralty regulations on the subject, but it is essential that he should know something of the

construction of the various parts of a vessel, and the best manner of ventilating those parts; the position of the machinery and the best manner of loading the stores.

3. The normal regulations may often have to be modified by imperative local conditions. The timber to be applied to the fittings must, and can only, be the best timber available on the spot, and the dimensions laid down may have to be greatly varied in order to meet the strength of that timber. The execution of the work can only be accomplished by the best available local carpenters, where the best available may be but very inferior workmen.

4. Speaking generally as to the class of ships, those of large capacity (5,000 tons and over) are most suitable to the requirements of horse transport owing to their facilities for carrying large water supply, which is a very important consideration in relation to the health of the cargo.

5. It is never safe to accept (as her real carrying capacity) any estimate drawn from the *plan* of a ship. It requires actual personal inspection by the responsible officer in order to arrive at an accurate conclusion on this point, for it is then only that ventilation, the course of steam pipes, the position of machinery, and the storage of spare gear can be investigated.

6. The main points to be noted in a ship destined to carry remounts are :—

(a) That she should carry the largest cargo consistent with safety, leaving 5 per cent. of spare stalls.

(b) That the fittings should be strong and present no dangerous surface.

(c) That the comfort of the cargo is ensured.

(d) That the ventilation, especially that of dead corners, is efficient.

(e) That electric light should be used in preference to any other.

(f) That the breadth of the alleyways at a minimum of 6 feet be maintained throughout the ship.

(g) The capacity and arrangement of the holds.

(h) That the brows should be strong, the angle of descent not unsafe, and that horses' heads should be protected from injury when descending.

(i) That the bracing and other fittings should depend for support on none but the *permanent* fixtures of the ship, and the solidity of the same should be insured.

(j) That the fixture of feeding troughs (which should be preferably of metal) is substantial.

(k) That the rope ties are sufficiently long (5 feet at least).

(l) That the water supply is detachable from the ship's engines and capable of being worked by hand in case of a breakdown.

(m) That no horses should be carried on poops or topgallant forecastles.

(n) That no horse should stand against a bulkhead or anywhere close to a steam-pipe.

(o) That the amount of surplus forage necessary to be carried, and the stowing of same, has been carefully provided for. This may be estimated at 1½ days per week for each week of the voyage.

7. In addition to the suitability of the freight ship, the remaining important factors governing the punctual and efficient delivery of remounts to the theatre of war are :—The correct estimation of the distances and of the speed of the individual ship; the climatic conditions relating to the time of year; the carriage of sufficient forage and water to cover accidents and delays ; and the efficient service of the conducting officers and muleteers.

8. The scales of feeding on remount ships is published by the Admiralty.

2. *Personnel on freight ships.*

1. The term muleteer is applied to all attendants in charge of animals on a remount freight ship, and their selection is of great importance.

2. Losses on board ship are mainly due to want of discipline, and the ignorance and unsuitability of the muleteers when they are engaged locally in foreign countries. Mutinous conduct at sea must have a bad influence on

the health and condition of the cargo, the delivery of which in a healthy and well-conditioned state is of the utmost importance.

3. *Attendants (horses).*	*Attendants (mules).*
1 head foreman.	1 head man for every 25 attendants.
1 assistant foreman for every 100 horses.	
1 attendant for every 10 horses.	1 attendant for every 20 mules.
2 carpenters in addition to ship's carpenters.	

4. Under the above conditions the engagement of the remainder of the muleteers (1 man for 10 horses, or for 20 mules) might without risk be left to the British Consul at the foreign port, subject to the opinion in each case of the remount officer.

5. It is essential that the head foreman should be a thoroughly competent and experienced cattleman, as energetic supervision is required. The 10 foremen should be rough and ready handymen, not subject to sea sickness, and trained to discipline, and able to make men work. It would be advantageous that these men should remain on the same ship during her service for the campaign ; they would form at all times a reliable backbone to the muleteers, and the foremen would be interested in the cleanliness and disinfection of their ship, whether full or empty. They should be paid a small bonus "per capita" on horses landed in condition ; 1 foreman could supervise 100 horses, and therefore some 10 men.

6. The foremen having risky work to do, the number should not be cut down to the lowest limit, in order to provide for accidents to one or more of their number.

7. Coloured men are generally better muleteers than the white men who offer themselves for engagement abroad; but if both races are embarked, each should be quartered separately in the ship, in the interests of discipline.

8. The question of a rate of pay in the engagement of muleteers is always a difficulty ; what is required is, to obtain competent men at a fair local rate of wages ; but as the men are signed on by the "boarding masters," it may not be effectual to offer high wages in order to get good men, because the "boarding masters" have it always in their power to secure to themselves the advantages of good pay, and nevertheless to furnish any vagrants they may be able to get hold of at a lower rate. The low standard of a majority thus engaged will act as a deterrent, and keep from joining, the better class of men at first. But when the work of the commission has been well established, the remount officers themselves will be able to note, and to bring about the re-engagement of men who have been known to have done good service on previous voyages. This matter will always require very careful watching on the part of the remount staff.

9. There is much to be said in favour of the conducting officer and the veterinary surgeon being attached permanently to the ship (as well as the foremen), in order that they may superintend the disinfection of the ship on the return journey, to take in a fresh cargo.

ADMIRALTY SPECIFICATION FOR FITTING TO BE CARRIED OUT BY OWNERS.

3. *Dimensions of stalls.*

	ft.	in.
Maximum length in the clear between breast rail and haunch board ...	8	0
(*Not less than maximum length to be given where possible.*)		
Minimum length in the clear between breast rail and haunch board ...	7	0
Passage between two rows of stalls, clear between breast rails, not less than	6	0
Breadth between parting boards in the clear, not less than ...	2	4*
Height of the parting boards from platform to top edge	3	9
Height of breast rail from platform to top edge	3	9

* 5 per cent. of the total number to be 2 feet 8 inches in the clear.

4. *Fittings on exposed deck.*

1. *The front stanchions* should be 6 inches by 4 inches, spaced 2½ feet apart, centre to centre, the height of same to be 8 feet from ship's deck. In way of horses' heads, stanchions to be covered with zinc 9 B.W.G. as may be required. Heels to be secured by a cant, 6 inches by 4 inches, fastened to the deck with a ⅝-inch nut and screw or tapped bolt, one to every 5 feet, and a ⅝-inch nut and screw bolt through heel of stanchion and cant. If on wood deck to be secured with ⅝-inch coach screws.

A staple for a hay net to be fastened to each front stanchion.

2. *Rear stanchions.*—To be 6 inches by 4 inches, spaced 2½ feet apart, centre to centre, the height to be 7 feet 2 inches from deck.

These stanchions to be thoroughly secured in position by means of iron clamps fitted to bulwark rail or rails. Stop to be arranged on back of stanchions to prevent their rising. Heads of stanchions to be cross-tied not less than every 15 feet, and as required by Inspector. Heels to be secured same as front stanchions.

3. *Roof rafters.*—To be 4½ inches by 3 inches, bolted to front and back stanchions. All roof rafters to be carried 2 feet past front stanchions and 6 inches past back stanchions.

Along upper end of front and back stanchions a 4 inches by 3 inches fore and after to be run. These fore and afters to be nailed to stanchions, and to be secured, in addition, with a ½-inch nut and screw bolt, through every second stanchion.

4. *Roof.*—To be 1½-inch tongued and grooved, and carried 2 feet past front stanchions and 6 inches past back stanchions, same as rafters, and to be covered with new No. 2 canvas, painted with three coats of oil paint.

5. *Back sheathing.*—Stalls to have tongued and grooved sheathing, 2 inches thick, to a height of 4 feet up from the deck and 1½ inches thick above. Sheathing to be nailed on to front of stanchions.

6. *Dung ports.*—To be cut in back sheathing where considered necessary, size about 24 inches by 24 inches.

7. *Breast rail.*—To be 10 inches by 3 inches, with upper third covered with zinc not less than 9 B.W.G. Breast rail to be scored 1½ inches at each end on the lower part over the iron cleat, so as to prevent the board from shifting fore and aft; a swinging stop of approved pattern to be fitted above breast rails on front of stanchions to prevent boards from lifting up out of place. The breast rails may be fitted in lengths to take two stalls.

8. *Cleats.*—Iron cleats ⅝ inch thick and 4 inches wide bolted on front of each front stanchion to take breast rail.

9. *Platforms.*—To be movable and, whenever possible, reversible, end for end, both ends being cut around front stanchions for this purpose. To be made with 1½-inch deal boards, the length of the stall with a 1-inch space left between them, secured with foot battens the width of the stall. Foot battens to platform to be of pitch or red pine four in number, rear batten to be 4 inches by 2 inches and placed 12 inches from rear end of stall (when stall is 8 feet long), but in no case to be less than 9 inches from the end, the other three battens to be 3 inches by 2 inches, the front one to be placed 9 inches from the end of platform, and the other two to be placed each one foot from the centre of platform. These battens to be chamfered and secured to platform by iron screws 2½ inches long, ½ inch diameter, well recessed below top of batten. All platforms are to have two battens underneath them—one under front foot batten and one under rear one 4 inches wide by 1 inch thick, to be secured with 6 screws. They are to be cut through at the spaces between the boards for drainage. Care should be taken that platforms fit on deck and do not rock.

10. *Parting boards.*—Parting boards, four in number, to be 9 inches by 2 inches with 3 inches clearance between each; 1½-inch parting pieces spiked near each end of board to give this clearance. These parting boards to slide in grooves at outer and inner ends, one set to each stanchion. Grooves may be machined (2-inch slot) out of solid wood or by attaching with screw nails 2 inches

by 2 inches battens on a 6 inches by 1½-inch backboard. Front of top parting board to be fitted with slip bolt, or an approved iron pin with ball head secured by chain to stanchions may be fitted into socket hole in stanchions just above top parting board. Back of top parting board to be fitted with wood stop to prevent parting boards rising.

11. *Troughs.*—To be of approved pattern, one to each stall, galvanized iron, about 1 foot 9 inches by 12 inches by 9 inches deep (not buckets).

12. *Two halter rings.*—Of approved pattern in positions as directed, and firmly secured.

Fittings under erections and in 'tween decks.

13. *Stanchions.*—Scantlings of stanchions, breast rail, platform, and parting boards as specified for fittings on exposed deck.

To be tightly wedged between decks, and to be secured at heads and heels as specified for exposed decks to prevent their shifting fore and aft, or athwartship, to Inspector's approval.

14. *Back of stalls.*—Ordinary cargo battens in 'tween decks to be filled in close with intermediate boards to a height of 12 inches above parting boards, and filled in on the upper part between frames. Where no cargo battens exist, the ship's side is to be lined up to a height of 12 inches above parting boards and top filled in as above.

15. *Ships fitted for cattle.*—Cattle ships fitted with cement decks to have portable floor pieces in lengths of two stalls laid close down on cement between outer two and inner two footlocks, and good drainage space to scuppers cut through footlocks and floor pieces under parting boards.

16. *Drainage.*—A passage 18 inches wide is to be left opposite every scupper, and where scuppers drain into the bilge, or are fitted with storm valves, they are to be covered with a fine rose. Sufficient number of scuppers to be cut in all 'tween decks and under all erections. As a general rule, a 4-inch scupper every 25 feet of erections will be found sufficient. All scuppers to have the word "scupper" painted on ship's side immediately above them in not less than 6-inch letters with the addition of the words "This Scupper is for Urine and not for Dung" underneath. Holes 9 inches by 2 inches to be cut out under front cants where necessary for the purpose of allowing the urine from amidship stalls to drain into the scuppers, and holes 6 inches by 2 inches under the rear and front cants of all amidship stalls, and under the rear cant of all upper deck side stalls.

17. *Water service.*—A permanent water service pipe to be fitted to all horse decks carried fore and aft. A cock is also to be fitted at each side at the following stations:—At after end of forecastle, fore and after ends of bridge deck, and at poop front on upper decks and at similar positions on shelter decks, with an additional cock in alleyway on each side. In 'tween decks of ordinary length a cock is to be fitted at each side, at forward and after end of each compartment. Special care to be taken that water service can be supplied from at least two independent pumps in the engine room in case of breakdown.

18. *Side lights.*—In long deck erections to be spaced not more than 16 feet apart, and in 'tween decks spaced about 12 feet apart.

19. *Wind scoops* of approved pattern to be fitted to all side lights.

20. *Electric light or candle lamps.*—To be fitted in erections, and in 'tween decks of sufficient number to give ample light; where candle lamps are fitted they are to be of approved pattern and hung on proper hooks. As a rule all ships carrying remounts will be required to be electrically lighted, and the dynamo will be required to be of force enough to carry out the entire service of lighting the ship and of working the fans at full power simultaneously.

21. *Ventilation.*—All erections (not necessarily enclosed) and all 'tween decks are to have ventilators of sufficient size and number, with their cowls carried clear above top fittings, besides which, all 'tween decks to have mechanical ventilation by means of fans, or other approved method, so as to

draw all foul air from the after end and, or if necessary, from the fore end of each compartment, and exhaust same at the top exposed deck.

22. *Windsails.*—Thirty inches diameter, with large mouth (square head preferred), to be supplied and fitted, at least two to each 'tween deck compartment, and where required in erections.

Conveyance in holds.

23. When it is found desirable to carry horses in the holds, which should only be done where the ship is specially suitable and ample head room can be secured, the stanchions should be first fitted from the bottom of the ship to the deck above, and coal stowed through the hold around them, and a wooden platform $2\frac{1}{2}$ inches thick laid on top of the coal, in no case less than 10 feet from the deck above, and more, when possible, up to 15 feet. Foot battens to be secured to floor inside the stalls as on ordinary platforms. The coal takes the drainage. The ship's side should be lined as in other decks, and a 12-inch bevelled board secured to the platform, to lean at an angle against the lining to allow for the settling of the coal.

The dimensions of stalls and scantlings to be according to specifications. Horses should not be stowed more than 15 feet before and abaft the hatch. Two 18-inch ventilators, with cowls, should be fitted at each end of the hold. Water service and lights to be as on other decks. No stalls to be erected amidships.

General.

24. A pharmacy to be built, size about 6 feet square, of 3-inch stanchions and 1-inch boarding. Spaces to be left between the boarding of top half for light and air. A door to be fitted, provided with hanging lock.

Shelves with face battens to be fitted, as directed, around the bulkheads. Also bottle racks and a broad shelf, 2 feet 9 inches from deck, for dispensing.

25. Five per cent. spare stalls are to be fitted in addition to the number of horses fitted for. Two per cent. to be fitted with slinging bars. The bars to be pitch or red pine, 4 inches by $3\frac{1}{2}$ inches, running fore and aft between the stanchions, with dumb sheaves worked on them, four to each front and two to each rear bar for each stall. The centre of front bar to be 18 inches from front stanchion, the rear one to be 3 feet from the front bar, centre to centre. These bars to be kept as high as possible, supported by and bolted to fir rails, 8 feet long by $4\frac{1}{2}$ inches by 3 inches, secured to stanchions by $\frac{5}{8}$-inch bolts and nuts. Heads of bolts to be smoothly rounded, ends to be cut off flush with the nuts and covered with wooden caps carefully smoothed off.

Two belaying cleats of $\frac{5}{8}$-inch iron are to be screwed to front of each stanchion of the slinging stalls, 18 inches and 5 feet 6 inches from the heel of stanchion respectively, for belaying the falls of the hammocks.

Finish.

26. All timber coming in contact in any way with the animals is to be well planned, smoothed, rounded, and neatly chamfered off.

27. Every stall to be numbered and all detachable parts to bear the same number as the stall to which they belong. Each set of parting boards to be also lettered A, B, C, D, beginning with A at the bottom.

28. *Stalls on exposed decks.*—Forward and after ends of rows of all stalls on exposed decks to be close sheathed full depth, with $1\frac{1}{2}$ inches tongued and grooved, upper portion of this to hinge down, and the ends to be made portable where required. Canvas screens to be fitted from outer edge of top of roofing to deck cants with lashings, &c., complete; these lashings also to tie screens when rolled up. Screens are to be hung in front of all stalls on the weather decks, as also at all ends of the centre stalls adjoining hatches on next deck below.

29. Brows are to be constructed to allow of shipping all horses; these brows to be of easy descent from upper to main and all other decks, and are

to be taken out on board the vessel. Brows to have strong sparred sides (not more than 3 inches spaces between spars); also in way of each fitting, &c., on deck ; when more than 6 inches high, small permanent brows to be fitted where it is intended to walk horses.

30. *Workmanship.*—All workmanship, material, and general arrangement of the stalls to pass the Inspector appointed, who may make any reasonable alterations in this specification while the work is in progress. Workmanship to be carried out in first class manner.

5. *Report of inspection of remount horse freight ship* ....

1. A first inspection of every freight ship will be held one day before the sailing of the vessel by a naval officer, a remount officer, and a veterinary officer, who will report as follows :—

    i. Number of horses shipped or to be shipped.
    ii. Has specification for fitting, &c., been carried out in a satisfactory manner ?
    iii. Are there 5 per cent. spare stalls ?
    iv. Are 2 per cent. of stalls fitted with slinging bars ?
    v. Ventilation of horse decks, if satisfactory.
    vi. Drainage of horse decks, if efficient.
    vii. Is water service for horses complete ?
    viii. Electric lighting. Are decks well lit ?
    ix. Number of windsails provided.
    x. Arrangements for supply of forage, if satisfactory.
    xi. Are all the articles in outfit and forage scale provided ?
    xii. Veterinary medicines, &c., if on board.
    xiii. Forage, &c., if examined by military authorities and found to be of good quality.
    xiv. Are horse brows provided for use on board ?
    xv. Is suitable accommodation provided for the remount officer, veterinary officer, and shoeing smiths ?
    xvi. Number of attendants. Have proper arrangement been made for messing, sleeping, cooking, and necessary sanitary provision for them ?
    xvii. Boats. Can they readily be lowered and hoisted up ?
    xviii. Fire. Precautions against fire and for extinguishing the same, if satisfactory.

2. A final inspection will be held immediately before the sailing of the vessel by the officers referred to above, who will report as follows :—

    i. Name of remount officer in charge.
    ii. Name of veterinary officer.
    iii. Number of horses shipped.
    iv. Is the width of passage between any two rows of stalls less than 6 feet ?
    v. Is ship in all respects ready for sea ?

3. These reports will be dated and signed by the officers carrying out the inspections, who will add any further general remarks desirable.

APPENDIX IX.

BOOKS AND FORMS REQUIRED BY OFFICERS OF REMOUNT COMMISSIONS.

Supplied by the War Office.

1. King's Regulations.
2. Admiralty Transport Regulations.
3. Allowance Regulations.
4. Field Service Regulations, Part II (Organization and Administration).
5. Remount Regulations.
6. Animals and Harness Manual.
7. Travelling claims (for home and abroad).
8. A small supply of unstamped foolscap and letter paper and envelopes.

Additional, for officer commanding the commission only.

9. Forms of accounts, depôts and other states, reports, &c., for use in the commission, to be reprinted as required in the country to which he proceeds.

10. Copy of ship's charter and Admiralty Maintenance Form.

11. A pattern of the brands to be used.

12. A pattern head collar for use on board ship.

NOTE.—All letters and reports are to be written plainly on foolscap paper, on one side only, and should be as brief as is possible consistent with perfect clearness. All that are not secret should, if possible, be typed. Clear distinction is to be made in reports between matters of opinion and matters of fact.

APPENDIX X.

SPECIAL FORMS USED BY REMOUNT COMMISSIONS.

A.

Army Form A 2045.

ACCOUNT—HORSE-PURCHASING COMMISSION.

N.B.—Subjects (*a*) and (*b*) are to be accounted for on separate forms, the headings of the various columns to be entered according to local necessity.

(*a*) Stores (including Veterinary Medicines); or (*b*) Supplies (*e.g.*, Forage, &c.).

Receipts.						Issues.					
Date.	No. of Voucher.					Date.	No. of Voucher.				
Total receipts... ...	...					Total issues	...				
Total issues	...										
Remaining	...										

(Signature)...............................

(Date).............................

B.

Army Form A 2004.

Station...

Date...

Depôt or Corps..

ANIMAL ACCOUNT (Remount Services).

Receipts.

No. of Voucher.	Date of Receipt.	From whom received.	Number of Animals.							Remarks.
			Horses.	Cobs.	Mules.	Oxen.	Donkeys.	Camels.	

Issues.

No. of Voucher.	Date of Issue.	To whom issued, or how disposed of.	Number of Animals.							Remarks.
			Horses.	Cobs.	Mules.	Oxen.	Donkeys.	Camels.	

Signature.............................

C.

(See Appendix III, para. 10 (Admiralty Maintenance Form).)

PARTICULARS OF EMBARKATION OF HORSES OR MULES IN THE FREIGHT SHIP "................................," AT THE PORT OF ...., FOR CONVEYANCE TO....................

Embarkation, &c.	Date.		First Class.		Government Shoeing Smiths or others.	Number of Animals Shipped.	
	Day.	Hour.	Name.	Rank.		Horses.	Mules.
Ship arrived at...............							
Reported ready to receive animals ... ... :							
Embarkation { commenced ... : completed ... :							
Ship sailed ... ... :							

For maintenance claim purposes—

No. Horses } were ready for embarkation here on
Mules } the...................... 19 .

NOTE.—This return should be forwarded to the Director of Transports, Admiralty, London, S.W., immediately on the sailing of a steamer engaged by the Transport Department to convey horses or mules from a foreign port. The following information should also be telegraphed to the Director of Transports ("Transports, London") on the vessel sailing:—

(Name of Ship) sailed.................. Mules or horses.................. Officers.................. Men..................

.... Remount Officer,

.............................., 19 .

APPENDIX XI.

FORMS OF AGREEMENT FOR HIRE OF LAND AND PREMISES BY A REMOUNT COMMISSION.

EXAMPLE No. 1.

AGREEMENT between .... and
....

Representing the British Government.

Form of Agreement for the Hire of Land, Buildings, &c., suitable for Central Corrals.

We agree to furnish to the British Government the use of
acres of land near   , for the purpose of grazing
and caring for thereon horses and mules, together with the use of 150 *box
stalls and 3 mule sheds,* and to feed with hay, corn, oats, and bran, all horses
and mules kept on said land by you for the British Government, at the rate
of   per head per day for horses, and
per head per day for mules.

We also agree to unload, and take to said land, and to take from said land
and load, all such horses and mules, when and as so directed by you, free of
all costs or charges to you.

You are, however, to keep, or pay for as kept under the above conditions,
on said land not less than   horses and mules per day for each day
from   , for the period of   months next
thereafter.

This agreement is to be binding upon us, and also binding upon you on
behalf of the British Government, and shall continue from the date of such
acceptance for a period of   months, viz., from   ,
inclusive, and unless terminated by   days' notice in writing, from either
party to the other, of a desire to terminate the same at the expiration of the
said   months, this contract shall continue until terminated by   days'
written notice from either party to the other of a desire to terminate the
same.

....
Lessor of Land, &c.

Accepted this   day of   ,   .

....
For British Government.
(done in duplicate).

EXAMPLE No. 2.

AGREEMENT between..and
....

Representing British Government.

Form of Agreement for the Hire of Land, Buildings, &c., suitable for Port Corrals.

This lease, made and entered into in the city of   , this
day of   witnesseth:—

That the (*person or company*), of (*city*), leases unto
                      , representing the British Government, all and singular the
premises at   , known as   , and the open
unenclosed grounds or spaces between the said sheds and the (*river, dock, or*

shore) save and excepting such portions of the same as may be covered by existing constructions of the party of the first part.

This lease is made for a term of   months, beginning on the   day of   ,   , and ending on the   day of   , , with the right in the party of the second part to renew same on the same terms and conditions for a period not to exceed   months thereafter, at his option, and with the further right to terminate said lease during the said period of   months, at any time, by giving   days' written notice, to take effect at the end of the ensuing month.

This lease is made under the condition, without which it would not have been made, that the party of the second part is to use the leased premises for holding, stabling, and maintaining horses and other cattle awaiting transportation across the seas, to have and maintain hospital accommodations and appliances, including a fire, which fire it is understood shall not be built closer than 20 feet from any shed or building, and, to that end, he shall have the right to enclose any part or all of the said open spaces above referred to, and he shall have free access to and across any other property of the party of the first part, and to and across its wharves, and free wharfage for ships coming to receive said cattle, and, to that end, the party of the first part guarantees to have and maintain at the said wharf at least 26 feet of water, and by dredging or otherwise to have said depth of water ready from and after the   ,   , in order that the party of the second part may utilize the same at once, and the party of the second part is accorded the right to take immediate possession of the leased premises, without obligation to pay rent therefor, and no rent is to be due by him except that which begins to accrue from and after the   . The wharf referred to is the wharf now existing at   , and this agreement contemplates that said wharf shall be maintained during the period of this lease.

The right is also accorded the party of the second part to erect a temporary pen capable of holding 200 *head of horses*, the same to remain during the term of this lease, but the party of the second part agree that an alley or space shall be left near said pen for the use of the party of the first part in the movement of freight on the wharf.

The party of the first part further guarantees, as a condition of this lease, to the party of the second part full and plenty drinking water through the pipes and pumps of the said party of the first part, sufficient for the use at all times of a minimum of 3,000 *head of horses*.

The party of the first part further agrees to switch (by the existing private line) from the nearest railway station promptly upon notice of all cars containing cattle, and to protect said cattle against damage by its delay or by its transport, and shall be entitled to charge therefor not more than   per car.

The party of the second part agrees to return the premises in like good order and condition as received, save and excepting the wear and tear and ordinary injury received by premises used for cattle, but he will leave the same as near broom clean as possible. It is well understood, however, that the party of the second part will not be responsible for fire or other injury to said building, nor is he under obligation to insure the said buildings.

In consideration of the premises, the party of the second part agrees to pay promply to the party of the first part the sum of   per month rent, beginning on the   day of   ,   , and on the first day of each and every succeeding month thereafter while the premises are occupied, and covenants and agrees further to pay for the use of the wharf and the privilege of the wharf as herein above established, the sum of   per head for cattle transported across the same to the ship's side.

The party of the first part covenants and agrees to maintain the party of the second part in possession for and during the whole term of this lease free from eviction or interference of all and singular the premises leased and the privileges granted in said lease.

In faith whereof the parties have hereunto set their signatures, in the city of   , on this   day of   ,   , in duplicate.

....

Lessor.

....

For British Government.

APPENDIX XII.

FORM OF ENGAGEMENT OF CIVILIAN VETERINARY SURGEONS

(On which can be based Similar Engagements made by Remount Officers Abroad).

EMERGENCY FORM.

To the Army Council.

I,   of   , being qualified to practise veterinary medicine and surgery, and being registered as a member of the Royal College of Veterinary Surgeons, hereby offer to serve as a Veterinary Surgeon to His Majesty's Forces on the following conditions, either at home or in ....

1. The period of my service hereunder shall commence from the date of my joining for duty, and shall continue until the expiration of 12 calendar months thereafter, or until my services are no longer required, whichever shall first happen.

2. My pay and allowances shall (subject as hereinafter appears) be the same as received by a..............................of the Army Veterinary Corps.

3. In addition to such pay and allowances, if sent to.............................., I shall receive a free passage from the United Kingdom to that country, together with travelling expenses from my residence to the port of embarkation ; and (subject as hereinafter appears) a similar free passage from.................. ....to the United Kingdom, together with travelling expenses from the port of disembarkation to my residence, at the end of the said period.

4. In the event of my being employed on conducting duty my pay shall be at the rate of £1 per day whilst on board ship in charge of remounts, or at 10s. a day only if not in charge of animals (*i.e.*, whilst proceeding to or returning from conducting duty), and a bonus on the following scale *in respect of animals landed in good condition*, of which the General Officer Commanding, or an officer acting on his behalf, shall be the sole judge :—

s.	d.					
2	0	a head if the losses do not exceed	1 per cent.			
1	6	,,	,,	,,	2	,,
1	0	,,	,,	,,	3	,,
0	6	,,	,,	,,	5	,,
0	3	,,	,,	,,	10	,,

Nil if the losses exceed 10 per cent.

5. During the said period I will devote my whole time and professional skill to my 'service hereunder, and wlll obey all orders given to me by Commissioned Military or Naval Officers, or by the Permanent Veterinary Officers.

6. In case I shall in any manner misconduct myself, or shall be (otherwise than through illness or unavoidable accident) unfit in any respect for service hereunder, of which misconduct or unfitness the general or other officer under

whom I am immediately serving shall be sole judge, such superior officer shall be at liberty from and immediately after such misconduct or unfitness to discharge me from further service hereunder, and thereupon all pay and allowances hereunder shall cease.

Dated this   *day of*   , 19

.....................................(*here sign*)

Witness to the Signature of the said

....

............................(*Witness*).

Engagement recommended

....................................D.G.A.V.S.

Accepted on behalf of the Army Council,

....

Director of Remounts.

INDEX.

757

ND - #0525 - 270225 - C0 - 195/125/6 - PB - 9781908487766 - Matt Lamination